Fairy-Tale
SUCCESS

Fairy-Tale SUCCESS

★

A GUIDE TO

Entrepreneurial Magic

ADRIENNE ARIEFF & BEVERLY WEST

Avon, Massachusetts

Published by
Adams Media, a division of F+W Media, Inc.
57 Littlefield Street, Avon, MA 02322. U.S.A.
www.adamsmedia.com

ISBN 10: 1-4405-7517-7
ISBN 13: 978-1-4405-7517-4
eISBN 10: 1-4405-7518-5
eISBN 13: 978-1-4405-7518-1

Printed in the United States of America.

10   9   8   7   6   5   4   3   2   1

Cinderella story excerpts from "Cinderella; or, The Little Glass Slipper," Andrew Lang, *The Blue Fairy Book*, 5th ed. (London: Longmans, Green, and Co., 1891), pp. 64–71; Lang's source: Charles Perrault, *Histoires ou contes du temps passé, avec des moralités: [Contes de ma mère l'Oye]* (Paris: Chez Claude Barbin, 1697); and from Jacob and Wilhelm Grimm, *Kinder- und Hausmärchen*, 1st ed. (Berlin: Realschulbuchhandlung, 1812), v. 1, no. 21. Translated by D.L. Ashliman. © 1998.

This publication is designed to provide accurate and authoritative information with regard to the subject matter covered. It is sold with the understanding that the publisher is not engaged in rendering legal, accounting, or other professional advice. If legal advice or other expert assistance is required, the services of a competent professional person should be sought.

—From a *Declaration of Principles* jointly adopted by a Committee of the American Bar Association and a Committee of Publishers and Associations

Cover design by Sylvia McArdle.

This book is available at quantity discounts for bulk purchases.
For information, please call 1-800-289-0963.

Contents

★

Acknowledgments

I would like to thank Beverly West for always making books more fun and inspiring! Thank you to our wonderful agent Stephany Evans at FinePrint Literary Management and our editors Christine Dore and Laura Daly at Adams Media, who helped us turn this book into a movement for young women to follow their hearts and entrepreneurial spirit. We Heart YOU.

A massive thank-you to the hundreds of teens and young women who shared their learnings, inspirations, and successes in life.

Colleagues, family, and friends, what would I do without you and your support?! Extra thanks to Maja, Erica, Dorka, Michelle C & H, Lisa, Sora, Alex P, Sasha, Nicole, Haimes, Chloe, Lydia, Natalia, Clara, Catherine, Regina, and last but not least the incredibly talented Sophie Sieck for helping me at the eleventh hour on several occasions. Also, I would like to thank my two very inspiring fairy godmothers, Patricia Hale and Allison Arieff, for always giving me sound and thoughtful advice.

Dad, I love you. Alex, Emma, and India, you are "my noon, my midnight, my talk, my song."

—Adrienne

A very special thanks to my coauthor Adrienne Arieff, one of my very favorite dance partners at the royal ball, who is always a delight to work with, even when the clock is striking twelve. Thanks also to our insightful and inspired editors Christine Dore and Laura Daly for making this project such a fairy-tale success. Special thanks too, to our agent Stephany Evans at FinePrint for staying by our side through this adventure, and to Becky Vinter, for her early insight and determination to make this dream come true.

Many, many thanks to all of the inspiring young women who have contributed their stories and their words of wisdom to this book. You are all awe-inspiring. And finally, thanks to my husband Jason, for being my happily ever after.

—Beverly

Dedications

To the late Carol Arieff—a fearless entrepreneur who inspires me daily. —Adrienne

To all of the fairy godmothers in my life, including Marilyn Knox, Ellen Rees, Pam Conway, and Billee Howard. —Beverly

INTRODUCTION

Cinderella, CEO

In Cinderella's timeless fairy tale—the classic version, not the popular movie interpretation—she's saddled with quite a few obstacles to finding her "happily ever after." She's got to contend with a wicked stepmother, two wicked stepsisters, an absent father, a deceased mother, and a *really* lousy job. Plus, she is basically grounded for life. Poor Cinderella spends all day every day cleaning fireplaces, scrubbing the floors, and separating the beans from the lentils—not exactly sexy bullet points on a college or job application. And yet somehow Cinderella manages to get herself invited to the fashion event of the season, and emerges as the belle of the ball and the talk of the kingdom. She has pulled herself up by her bootstraps, gotten a little help from some friends, and exercised the power she found within herself long before the prince ever arrives on the scene.

In other words, Cinderella is no sleeping beauty who just passes out on a bed of roses and waits for the handsome prince to arrive. Cinderella is a self-determined and innovative entrepreneur, a born CEO with a killer marketing sense, and a great sense of herself. She designs and launches her own campaign to make her vision—a better life—a reality. Far from an irrelevant anachronism from a more magical and innocent, not to mention patriarchal, time, Cinderella is actually an icon for today's entrepreneurial age.

When you think about her that way, Cinderella the marketing genius has a lot in common with the young and inspirational CEOs who are taking the business world by storm these days, sometimes before the age of fifteen!

Fairy-Tale Success is our blueprint for fairy-tale success using Cinderella's secrets in a modern-day business context. Complete with step-by-step instructions, suggestions, and advice from real-life Cinderella CEOs of today—from our top-notch advisory board—this is your plan for making your dreams come true and ruling your world with entrepreneurial awesomeness. Check out *http://fairytalesuccess.tumblr.com* to connect with other entrepreneurs following the same path as you!

Like Cinderella, today's successful young CEOs throw themselves into their work, always envisioning a brighter future. Thanks to their dedication, innovation, and vision, they are able to reveal a glittering glass carriage where before there had only been a pumpkin because they understand and employ the very same principles that Cinderella did. Those principles are just as applicable in today's business world as they are in storybooks. You'll find a list of Cinderella Principles at the end of each chapter in this book. These philosophies and strategies based on Cinderella's story will help you reach your goals, step by step.

Within these principles, you'll find keys to mastering such essential, lifelong skills as:

* ★ Communication
* ★ Creative Thinking
* ★ Decision Making
* ★ Money Management
* ★ Organization
* ★ Timing
* ★ Research
* ★ Sales Techniques
* ★ Public Relations
* ★ Publicity Tools
* ★ Team Building
* ★ Goal Setting
* ★ Focus
* ★ Diplomacy
* ★ Self-Discipline

No matter what line of work you end up in, these skills will always serve you well. Whether you're writing a blog, getting the word out about your fabulous new jewelry or fashion line, selling your one-of-a-kind handcrafts, launching a tech startup, or designing a new app that will take the world by storm, Cinderella's secrets to fairy-tale success will help you get find your own happy ending. To start, all you need is your "magic wand"—your belief in yourself.

Meet Our Advisory Board

These amazing women served as our "advisory board" for this book. They told us their stories—how they made their passions into successful real-life ventures. They (along with other young entrepreneurs and role models) offer plenty of advice throughout the book for up-and-coming Cinderella CEOs—what to do, what not to do, and how to find your happily ever after. Please visit *http://fairytalesuccess.tumblr .com* to learn more about each advisor, and to connect with other young entrepreneurs like you!

Michaela d'Artois

Michaela d'Artois is a journalist living in San Francisco, CA. Her career in fashion and writing was pretty much set from a young age, stemming from a strong need to express herself through the sartorial. When she realized her love for writing, and the energy she gained from meeting like-minded and creative people interested in fashion, her path decided itself. She works for several fashion blogs, including Refinery29 (*www.refinery29.com*), and is a featured stylist on several different fashion blogs.

Skyler Bouchard

Born and raised in Delaware, Skyler moved to New York in 2011 to pursue a bachelor's degree at NYU in broadcast journalism and media, culture, and communication. Since then, she started her own food blog (*www.foodbyskyler.com*), which led her to become the founder and editor-in-chief and founder of NYU's first culinary website, *NYU Spoon*, a branch of the national college food magazine website, *Spoon University*. Skyler has been working towards a career in the entertainment industry since her senior year in high school with a promotions internship at 99.5 WJBR radio, an editorial internship at *Bullett Magazine*, a writing internship at the *Daily Meal*, and a public relations internship at Hearst Magazines. She began working in the television industry her junior year of college, landing a production internship at *Entertainment Tonight* and *The Insider*, where she assisted with segment shoots in the field and worked with a variety of public figures, celebrities, editors, and specialists. She spent a spring semester as an entertainment news intern at CNN, where she had the opportunity to assist with production behind the scenes and conduct red carpet interviews. She recently spent the summer of 2014 working as a "Living Unit" intern at *NY1 News* and will continue on to graduate from NYU in the fall of 2014. Skyler is a passionate, hardworking self-starter and is always open to new experiences. She plans to further her career as a broadcast journalist and food blogger upon graduation.

Jamila Clay

Jamila Clay is a force in marketing. As an only child, she got her motivation from her family to make it in life. Through good old-fashioned love and support, they taught her how to be a confident individual. Jamila continues to thrive in various roles in marketing and PR. She credits her success and drive to her immediate family, who all have successful personal and professional lives. "When you grow up around confident, loving people, it sets the stage for wonderful things to happen."

Bernadette Coh

Bern Coh lives and works in San Francisco. After four years in technical recruiting at companies like Yahoo and Twitter, Bern joined Airbnb to launch their inaugural university recruiting program, which she currently runs as a technical recruiter. The first in her family to come to the United States, she studied women's studies and sociology at Loyola Marymount University. She's a fierce believer in mentorship and creating economic opportunity for young people from underrepresented communities. You can find her at *@berncoh*, where she tweets all day, mostly about what food she's eating or wants to eat soon.

Kit Hickey

Kit Hickey is the cofounder of Ministry of Supply (*www .ministryofsupply.com*), a menswear company out of MIT, which aims to re-create the way men think about business clothing. Sweat stains on dress shirts from perspiration is a nightmare for every professional working today. A handful of young MIT students believe they have engineered a shirt that will make this embarrassing mishap a thing of the past. Ministry of Supply is bringing the qualities of athletic gear and marrying them to business apparel—Under Armour meets Polo. Ministry of Supply launched its newest shirt, the Apollo, on Kickstarter.com, and it became the most-funded fashion project of all time, raising $430,000 from nearly 3,000 customers in forty countries. Founded in December of 2010 and launched in October 2013, Ministry of Supply's six founders Kevin Rustagi, Gihan Amarasiriwardena, Eddie Obropta Jr., Eric Khatchadourian, Kit Hickey, and Aman Advani have already seen over $13,000 in revenue since its launch.

Prior to Ministry of Supply, Hickey cofounded BiD Network USA, a nonprofit dedicated to helping entrepreneurs in emerging markets access venture capital funding. Her previous experience also includes doing investment banking work in San Francisco and London. Hickey earned a bachelor's degree from Colby College and completed some coursework in the MBA program at MIT's Sloan School of Business.

Daisy Jenks

Daisy Jenks started her own video production agency in London with her close friend Kitty when they were young teenagers. Starting out filming music videos on laptops for class, they have now filmed and produced more than 200 video projects for parties, film, weddings, and media events. She currently has her own successful video and film production company out of the UK, *www.jenksandco.tv.*

Weisi Kang

Weisi (pronounced *way-sah*) Kang (*kay-ng*) is a graduate of the University of California, Berkeley with a bachelor's degree in business administration and media studies. She was born in Beijing, China, and has since settled in California for almost fifteen years. She did not become passionate about marketing and social media until her senior year of high school when she did her capstone project on Disney's advertising strategy. Since then, she has taken on internships and job opportunities in PR, social media, and marketing in a variety of industries, including at *Dream-Row* (an online music magazine), Lives of Style (a broadcast fashion and lifestyle show), Epix (a premium cable channel owned by Viacom), and Medallia (customer experience management software company). Her website is *www .weisik.com.*

Erin Schrode

Erin Schrode is a young ecoRenaissance woman. As the "face of the new green generation," the cofounder of Teens Turning Green (*www.teensturninggreen.org*) promotes global sustainability, youth leadership, environmental education, and conscious lifestyle choices. Since 2005, her youth-led nonprofit has worked to raise public awareness about environmental and social responsibility for individuals, schools, and communities through education and advocacy—inspiring the transition from conventional to conscious living among high school and college students, as well as the greater public. After working in disaster response in Haiti, she founded and launched The Schoolbag, a youth education project to provide tools and materials for students in need, as well as initiate active citizenry and environmental stewardship. The program has reached more than 30,000 students in Haiti, in addition to deliveries in East Timor and South Africa.

This "incredible synthesizer and orator" speaks internationally and consults with corporations and organizations on Millennials, social consumption, digital tendencies, sustainability, and purpose to drive positive impact and better business. A "sustainability prodigy," Erin has been featured in and tapped as an expert for the *New York Times, Vanity Fair, SF Chronicle, NY Post, Seventeen* magazine, *Teen Vogue, National Geographic,* ABC, NBC, BBC, CNN, FOX, MTV, PBS, E!, AOL, and other multimedia outlets. The "juggernaut in the non profit and green world" hosts digital programs, leads events, and writes for *Huffington Post,* her own ecoRenaissance blog, Twitter, and others. An award-winning ecopreneur, Erin is the spokesperson for top organic and recycled brands, US Ambassador to One Young World, and as the White House said, "a dynamic, passionate and ambitious young woman committed to creating big change everywhere she goes." She recently graduated from New York University as a prestigious DEANS Scholar, spending terms abroad in the Middle East, West Africa, South America, and Europe. Having visited more than sixty countries, Erin has developed a keen global perspective and hopes to inspire her peers to take action and make the world a more sustainable and just place for future generations. Her website is *www.erinschrode.com*.

Sophie Sieck

Sophie Sieck (*@itsprincesssoph*) found a natural fit in the exploding field of public relations and digital media through her interest in reading, social media, and always being up on trends! Based in the Bay Area, Sophie worked with multiple tech startups and wrote for various blogs (including her own). She found her home blogging and working at a PR agency focusing on social media and press relations for companies such as Adidas and Method. She attributes her career successes to the experience she gained early on, jumping in and not listening to others who held her back, and the continuous support of her family.

Amy Zhang

Amy Zhang is an Electrical Engineering and Computer Science (EECS) major at UC Berkeley. Her career direction in STEM (science, technology, engineering, and math) was obvious at an early age given her love for math, science, and Legos, and was confirmed by her experience in the FIRST Robotics international high school competition. She came to Berkeley as Engineering Undeclared but eventually settled in EECS after hearing a very enthusiastic CS professor speak about his passion. Upon arrival at college, she joined the Society of Women Engineers as a freshman and is now the president of her collegiate section. She has just accepted a job at Google as a software engineer.

Aza Ziegler

California native and Brooklyn-based designer Aza Ziegler's career in fashion started at an early age. Born into a family of artists and creative thinkers, Aza was encouraged to embrace her creativity and express herself artistically. At age twelve, she was featured in *Women's Wear Daily* for her one-of-a-kind skirt line. Now, ten years later, Aza graduated from the Pratt Institute while simultaneously releasing her first SS14 collection at Center 548 in New York City, under her own name, Aza Maria Lucia Ziegler (*http://aza zeigler.com*). Playful, fearless, and adventurous are words not only to describe Aza herself but her fanciful, effortless designs and imaginative textiles. Greatly inspired by her roots out west, Aza does not fail to transition from west to east and everywhere in between. Zeum magazine just named her "one to watch."

CHAPTER 1

Reveal Your Noble Roots

★

EMBRACE YOUR VALUE

*O*nce there was a gentleman who married, for his second wife, the proudest and most haughty woman that was ever seen. She had, by a former husband, two daughters of her own, who were, indeed, exactly like her in all things. He had likewise, by another wife, a young daughter, but of unparalleled goodness and sweetness of temper, which she took from her mother, who was the best creature in the world.

No sooner were the ceremonies of the wedding over but the stepmother began to show herself in her true colors. She could not bear the good qualities of this pretty girl, and the less because they made her own daughters appear the more odious. She employed her in the meanest work of the house.

The poor girl bore it all patiently, and dared not tell her father, who would have scolded her; for his wife governed him entirely. When she had done her work, she used to go to the chimney corner, and sit down there in the cinders and ashes, which caused her to be called Cinderella. However, Cinderella, notwithstanding her coarse apparel, was a hundred times more beautiful than her sisters, although they were always dressed very richly.

Who Are You?

Before Cinderella even begins to think about the possibility of gate-crashing a royal ball and winning a place on the dance floor of power, she first has to wipe away the ash and soot of other people's negative perceptions of her and find out who she really is. She needs to define herself outside of her wicked stepmother and stepsisters and her current lot in life.

Only when Cinderella truly knows who she is and what she stands for does she begin to come up with an idea and construct an effective plan for launching herself into the world and finding her fairy-tale success. In Cinderella's day, this was no easy task—she lived in a completely class-defined economy with no chance of advancement without the proper pedigree. Sure, society is different today, but those obstacles are still very real. Unearthing your real self is the first step to creating a business as amazing as you are.

Indulge Your Curiosities

If you can't immediately point to any one skill, talent, or way of thinking that really sets you apart, don't despair. Everybody, even Cinderella, has a little bit of self-discovery to do before they can realize where their treasure lies. It takes some thought, some leaps of faith, some unflinching honesty, and some sustained effort to figure out what you're good at, what you're not cut out for, where your true talents lie, and what will make you truly happy in the long-term.

Figuring out where your personal and professional destinies lie involves a lot of trial and error and will evolve, over time, as you delve deeper and deeper into your adventure.

Ask Yourself Questions

The best way to begin the process of discovering yourself is to be curious about the world around you and the world inside you. You'll do an exercise on this shortly, but for now, here are a few big-picture questions that can help you think about the whole you:

- ★ What do you care about?
- ★ What are you willing to stand up for?
- ★ When are you the happiest?
- ★ What types of people are you drawn to?
- ★ What can you absolutely not tolerate?

These questions can help you pinpoint specific areas that you are passionate about. Whether you identify with a social movement, a religion, a particular business or trade, or a personality trait (such as helping others), your fairy-tale success will likely have its roots in one of these areas. Passion leads to motivation, which leads to dedication and success.

The Path Is Not Straight

This process also involves some research and independent study. Be curious and learn as much as you can, wherever you can, about the subjects that interest you. Perhaps even more important, don't be afraid to explore topics that don't interest you right away. Sometimes it isn't until you spend a little bit of time thinking about something that it begins to capture your imagination. You might learn something new, meet people unlike you, or discover a new passion—all of which will help you along your journey to success.

⋆⋆ Words of Wisdom from Fairy Godparents ⋆⋆

"How many cares one loses when one decides not to be something but to be someone."

—Coco Chanel, founder of House of Chanel

Be thorough. Don't leave any stone unturned. Go searching for your passions wherever you think they might be, and be willing to make a few wrong turns along the way. There are many Cinderella CEOs who thought they wanted to do one thing and wound up discovering that they were meant for something else entirely. For example, Coco Chanel originally wanted to sing and dance on the stage but ended up opening a little hat shop that became the world-renowned House of Chanel.

One of the great things about being young is that you have the time and the freedom to try on all different sorts of hats to see how they make you feel. Remember, it's only through experiencing different ideas, people, activities, hobbies, and adventures that you can begin to narrow down what suits you and what sends you running for the door. You are living in a world of "first times," ones you will never forget. Appreciate and take advantage of the blank canvas of your life. You will be amazed at the magnificent colors and textures that wind up there once you pick up the brush and start creating.

Take the "What's Your Happily Ever After?" Quiz

One of the best ways to start to develop the self-awareness you will need to become a Cinderella CEO is to take the "What's Your Happily Ever After?" quiz. This will help you home in on and record what you really enjoy doing, being, and sharing. Keep track of your answers in a blog, a vlog, or a handwritten journal. Feel free to use drawings, inspiration you clip out of magazines, or your Pinterest board—but most importantly, use your own voice to develop a portrait of who you are and what you stand for. This can give you some important clues about what your "happily ever after" might look like.

Ask yourself the following questions, and don't be afraid to branch out and create your own follow-up questions you think may help you. Think carefully about your answers and be as specific and detailed as you possibly can. Most importantly, don't censor yourself. Be passionate, be ironic, be thoughtful, be silly, be *you*. Understanding how you feel about the matters covered in these questions will help you get a handle on who you are, what you are passionate about, and what you believe in. Your answers will be a great help in determining the career or lifestyle you want to pursue.

Keep your journal with you once you embark on your journey, and add to it when you discover new passions or run into bumps in the road. When you're having doubts and worrying that your carriage might turn back into a pumpkin at any second, look back at your journal and remind yourself of what got you to the ball in the first place. Add new thoughts, ideas, or lessons learned so you can see how far you've come while still keeping an eye on your future. Your journal should be a living, breathing, and evolving mission statement for your life, so take it out once in a while to update it.

⋆⁺ Words of Wisdom from Fairy Godparents ⋆⁺

"I'm just like everyone else. I check pockets. I roll socks. I give tips. I skip pages. I fall asleep. I turn it off. I give directions. I scroll down. I make sure it's even. I leave it out. I lock eyes. I write it down. I say thank you. I walk away. I pretend laugh. I for real cry. I say I voted. I wonder if he really loves me. I'm not Ingrid Bergman, or Simone de Beauvoir. I'm nobody of note. I'm Yokoo, and I make scarves, some of which are chunky."

—Yokoo Gibraan, knitting wunderkind and Etsy star

Question #1: What kinds of people make you happy?

Think about the people that you have been drawn to in your life. What do they have in common?

- ★ Do you like people who are outspoken, gregarious, and the life of the party?
- ★ Or do you prefer quieter wallflowers who blossom once they get comfortable?
- ★ Do you prefer formal folks or people who are relaxed and down-to-earth?
- ★ Do you like spending time with people who are younger, older, or your own age?
- ★ Do you like free spirits or people who follow the rules?
- ★ Who do you admire and respect?
- ★ Who makes you mad?

★ If you were throwing a royal ball, who would you invite?

The answers to these questions will help you determine who you might work well with, who you can learn from, and who you should probably avoid as you follow your dreams.

_____

_____

_____

_____

_____

_____

_____

_____

Question #2: What kinds of places make you happy?

Think about your favorite places—whether you've lived there or simply visited. What did they have in common?

★ Do you like the beach and lots of sun or do you like mountains with lots of snow?

★ Do you prefer being indoors or outdoors most of the time?

★ Do you like big cities or small towns?

★ Do you like interiors that are traditional or do you prefer more modern surroundings?

★ Do you like lots of shops and museums and restaurants, or do you like wide-open natural settings with no buildings as far as the eye can see?

★ If you could design your ideal setting for life and work, what would that setting be?

As they say: location is everything. If you don't like the space where you live and work, you'll have a tough time enjoying anything! That's why it's important to try to figure out spaces you like and don't like. If you've only been exposed to one type of setting thus far in your life, consider traveling a little to experience something different. Travel can be expensive, but there are lots of ways to see other places inexpensively—visiting a potential college, going to a relative's house for a holiday, or taking a school-sponsored field trip.

_____

_____

_____

_____

_____

_____

_____

_____

Question #3: What kinds of activities make you happy?

Imagine your perfect day.

★ What would you do?
★ Would you get up early or sleep in?
★ Would you go biking or shopping with your friends or would you stay home alone and read a book?
★ Would you go out to eat at a fancy restaurant, visit a burger stand, or cook a meal for your family?
★ What are your hobbies?
★ What do you like to do to relax?
★ What activities completely absorb your attention?
★ What are the tasks that you do every day that make you feel the most useful, satisfied, fulfilled, and happy?

Often, the things that make you feel useful, satisfied, fulfilled, and happy are the things that you're the best at! The feeling of satisfaction comes from a job well done, which is made easier when you actually *enjoy* what you're doing. Finding out what activities make you the most fulfilled will help you narrow down what you're most interested in and what you will be happiest doing long-term. Choosing a career path that will make you happy will not only keep you focused and dedicated to the work you're doing, but it will also make your professional environment a place you want to be.

_____

_____

_____

_____

_____

_____

_____

_____

_____

_____

Question #4: What kind of culture makes you happy?

"Culture" is more than going to the opera. It's difficult to define, but it's a combination of the views that you and those around you have and the activities you like to take part in, or watch.

★ What kind of environment do you feel most comfortable in?
★ Do you like to go to parties and dances or do you prefer to have a visit with just one best friend?
★ What kind of music do you like?
★ What kinds of books do you read?
★ Would you rather go to a ballgame or a Broadway play?
★ Are you liberal or conservative?
★ Are you high-fashion or grunge?
★ Think about all of the varied influences that enrich your life every day. Where do you feel happiest, your most challenged, and most like your best self?

Defining your cultural preferences is important. Your own personal culture contributes a lot to the person you are becoming; it also helps you determine what kind of environment you will thrive in. Not every work environment is the same, and your "job culture" can really affect your happiness level on the job, as well as your productivity. More and more companies are beginning to operate with an open-office floor plan, for example. Many people find the option of constant socialization distracting, while others see it as a way to collaborate. These preferences will be an important part of determining your ideal office culture.

_____

_____

_____

_____

_____

_____

_____

_____

Question #5: What causes are you passionate about?

You probably have some issues—whether global or local—that are important to you on some level. Determining what's important to you will help you focus your work in a meaningful way.

★ What are you for?
★ What are you against?
★ Would you be more likely to attend a volunteer cleanup in the park, help feed the hungry, or volunteer at an animal shelter?
★ What are you concerned with globally?
★ What do you do locally?

Being passionate doesn't mean you have to storm the White House in a loud protest—whatever style you choose is fine. Believe it or not, no matter how old you are, your opinions and your voice are important. Passion also applies to many different areas; the question "What are you for?" can be answered many different ways. For example, you might say, "I am for floral patterns and Saturdays in the park, and I also believe all children should have access to an education and clean drinking water." No passion is too small. These continue to help you define your interests and pave your path to magic. Voice your opinion and take action on your passions—you never know where they might lead you.

_____

_____

_____

_____

_____

_____

_____

_____

Follow-Up Questions

If you're stumped on a particular question, take some time away from it and come back to it a week later. Ask those close to you what matters to them, and how they ended up living where they live, doing the work they do, or interested in specific causes. You want to be sure you're being true to *your* life above all, but sometimes you can get inspiration from people you trust and admire. Taking the time to ask your real-life role model what she's passionate about and what helped her discover her passions can be an incredible learning experience and a chance to make a lasting connection with someone involved in your field of interest.

Why Does Happiness Matter?

At this point, you might be asking yourself what all these questions have to do with trying to launch a business. The truth is, the things you love to do are usually the things that you do best. If you love making jewelry by yourself in your room on the weekends, you're probably pretty good at it by now and getting better every weekend. Maybe your jewelry is even becoming good enough for you to try to sell some custom pieces to your friends. That's what Shomari Patterson did—and those weekends gave birth to her company, Shamazzle's Dazzles.

✦ Words of Wisdom from Fairy Godparents ✦

"I know what you're thinking—'yet another Ackermann-struck kid, waxing (semi) eloquent about some show or some shoe, expecting us to give two shits and actually read.' I urge you to think again. I think Tom Ford owns Tom Hanks' ass, Coco Chanel epitomizes feminism, and Cathy Horyn deserves her own reality show."

—Arushi Khosla, founder of Fab Blab, now called Bohemian Like You

If you love fashion, you're probably always looking for ways to learn more about your passion and to incorporate it into your own sense of style. You may be learning how to sew or to create your own designs and you're getting better and better at it with each piece you make. If you love writing, you are probably spending a lot of time honing your craft and reading other writers who feed your imagination, just because you love it. Soon you will have a strong enough voice to share with others on a blog that could ultimately earn you a loyal readership, even a book deal!

Most people tend to think about work as something that you have to do for money. But as many Cinderella CEOs have discovered, it doesn't matter how successful you become if you can't stand what you are doing every day. Money really doesn't buy happiness, so if a career path or a business venture is going to lead to a happily ever after for you, it has to include the people, places, beliefs, and activities that make you feel comfortable, engaged, useful, and happy. Otherwise, what is the point?

If Cinderella had a Happily Ever After journal, she would have written that she had to find a way to somehow get herself to that royal ball, because she was born to be a princess. Who are you born to be?

Royal Role Model Q&A

Sophie Sieck
@itsprincesssoph

Tell us a little about your background.

I began my fairy-tale training during my sophomore year at the University of Arizona. As a political science major unsure of how involved I wanted to be in politics, I set out to look for other things that interested me. It was during this time that I found a social media internship with a local Bay Area nonprofit, Teens Turning Green.

Teens Turning Green was at a crucial point in their development, on the brink of launching their largest initiative yet, looking to gain interest from college-age students interested in "greening their lives." Since we all know how hard it is to successfully communicate with a large audience of eighteen- to twenty-one-year-olds, they needed help. I went to work, creating social channels for the Project Green Challenge, reaching out to eco-focused groups on all major universities across the country, and helping to organize sponsors such as The Container Store and Whole Foods to back the Project Green Challenge.

During this internship I found myself loving the exploding field of social media and I knew that is where I wanted to stay—and that is where I am today.

Do you have any words of wisdom to share with other young entrepreneurs?

Find your voice! Everything came together for me when I realized I had a voice through my writing. I realized I was funny and had a talent that could really make people respond and interact with each other. It was my outlet and it became something I turned into a profession.

What are your guilty pleasures?

Bad TV shows. I have a horrible addiction to Bravo. I also love *Diners, Drive-Ins and Dives*, you can never have enough Guy Fieri.

What's the best tip you've ever received on success?

Start early. That is the absolute best advice I have been given. There is a lot of competition in every field these days, which isn't a bad thing. But it means you have to work harder to get where you want to be. Have a clear idea of what direction you want to head in (it doesn't have to be an exact career), but if you like writing, like I do, then begin interning at your school newspaper, start a blog, or apply for an internship at your favorite magazine. Make sure you have something to show for yourself when you ultimately want to start your professional career that makes you stand out for what you love to do.

Can you share any advice on making a first endeavor in the world of business?

Don't worry, it will all be okay! Starting your first job is hard and it's stressful. Suddenly, you have responsibilities you have only observed during your internships and it's okay to have no idea what's going on for a second—this is your time to learn. Rise up to the challenge and ask questions. There is a reason that this company hired you, they saw something in you and they think you can do it. Nobody has time to put their faith in an employee they don't think can get the job done. Show them what you can do!

How have your parents helped you achieve success?

My father and stepmom were fantastic in supporting me. They moved me to New York from San Francisco for a summer to intern in PR and social media because that was my passion and they knew it would take me places. They supported my studies in Argentina and Spain and my dad was always there to proofread my work. Your parents are also great resources. My dad had worked in marketing for almost thirty years when I was ready to join the workforce and he had so much knowledge about the media and marketing industry. He put me in contact with many people who I am still in touch with today that have helped me in various ways through my career. My stepmother is actually the reason I was lucky enough to score one of my first interviews (and first job!) out of college. They may seem like a huge burden on your life now, but your parents are there to support you and they are definitely cooler than you think.

Is it scary to follow your heart?

It is scary, but it's even scarier to be stuck on a career path you don't want to be on. Remember, this is your future so it's time to listen to yourself. Do what makes you happy, not what makes you rich. Don't get distracted or discouraged by what is classified as a "glamorous" or "acceptable" career—what's in your heart is what's important! Now, more than ever, the job landscape is changing. Jobs that didn't even exist three years ago are becoming more and more important. Take fashion bloggers: they were the ones sitting in the front at all the shows during New York Fashion Week when not too long ago that would have been unheard of. It's scary, but who knows what may happen . . .

Turning Cinders into Silk

One of the lessons that Cinderella learns on her journey is that sometimes your best attributes can, on first glance, look a lot like trouble spots. The problems in Cinderella's life stem from the fact that she is different from her stepsisters. She is set apart by her hidden potential, flourishing unseen, deep within her. The fact that she's different does not make her very popular at the beginning of her story, but without those early conflicts she would never have blossomed into the royal princess she was always meant to be. Cinderella had a decision to make: accept the life that made her miserable, or rise up to the challenges in front of her. After years of dealing with her stepsisters and stepmother, Cinderella was ready to fight for her nobility. Her trouble spots gave her the strength to take what was rightfully hers!

CINDERELLA CEO PROFILE

Corianna and Brianna, AKA Coco and Breezy
Coco and Breezy
www.cocoandbreezy.com

Coco and Breezy developed their Grace Jones–meets–*Star Trek* signature style while working in a clothing store in their hometown of Metro Park, Indiana. The twins' meticulous ensembles, which took hours to create and made use of found objects such as bits of broken glass off the street, could literally stop traffic on their way to school in the morning, and not in a good way. They say that their Gladiator chic shades evolved because they wanted to avoid eye contact with people who were ridiculing them for the way they looked and dressed. Coco and Breezy believed in their signature style, even if nobody else did, and intentionally drawing on those elements that they knew set them apart in high school, the twins launched their own line of handmade accessories from home when they were just seventeen years old. A mere nine months later, Coco and Breezy were on their way to New York City to start designing their first line for the runways. Today, they are heading up their own international fashion accessory company, doing what they do best, only this time to cheers instead of jeers.

On their blog, they say: "God has a plan for all of us . . . He isn't just going to hand it . . . you have to seek it first." and "Your energy is your baby . . . don't let negativity take a piece of it . . . ((DEFINITION)) - When a person says something negative to you, don't take your extra energy out to get mad with that person. Your energy makes you. USE YOUR ENERGY TO TURN NEGATIVITY INTO A POSITIVE MATTER."

Building Your Business's Foundation with a Brand Signature

Once you have a firm handle on what you like to do, what is important to you, and what you want yourself and your business to stand for, it's time to capture everything you have learned about yourself into a "brand signature." A brand signature is the unmistakable stamp that you put on every single piece of content, product, promotion, or service that your business generates. You don't even have to know exactly what your business is yet—this signature will live with your work no matter which direction it takes. Your brand signature should include all of the qualities that you have identified in your Happily Ever After journal as being of vital importance to you. A brand signature isn't just about what you make or sell, but how you make it, how you sell it, and what you do with the money you generate.

Developing a brand signature means figuring out what, specifically, you are good at, what you want to provide or produce, as well as what you stand for, what you want to devote your time, love, and attention to, and what you wish to say to the world. Your brand signature should be concise and precise, and you should be able to articulate it in very few words, and then shout it everywhere you can, in thought, word, and deed. Be consistent! Brand consistency is everything at the beginning of a great venture and an authentic, well-thought-out, and consistently executed brand signature is the first step toward brand success.

If, for example, you feel strongly about the environment, your brand signature should always include eco-friendly practices, methods, and materials that support this aspect of your vision. Here are some examples of solid brand signatures.

- ★ **Method: People Against Dirty.** Method's brand signature comes from their commitment to creating cleaner, more environmentally friendly home products. They have a playful voice behind their "Clean Happy" slogan that reflects their brand personality.
- ★ **Nike: Just Do It.** Nike has done a great job of creating a brand signature that immediately comes to mind when you think of the brand name. It embodies their "all or nothing" athletic attitude and has reached beyond the Nike products to a larger lifestyle brand.
- ★ **Starbucks:** Starbucks has just about made the words "coffee" and "Starbucks" interchangeable. Their brand signature is in part their logo, but also their uniquely cozy coffee shops. Starbucks was the forerunner of the coffee shops that feel like your living room, and this made them stand out from the rest.

Examples of Cinderella CEOs' Brand Signatures in Action

Here are some examples of how your brand signature might come to life as you run your business like these other young entrepreneurs. Don't worry about thinking on a grand scale at first—small actions make a huge difference!

Jewelry Compassion Kits

A big part of Shomari Patterson's brand is about empowering young girls. So, every time she sells a piece of jewelry, Shomari donates what she calls a jewelry compassion kit to a home in Thailand for girls who were victims of human trafficking. The compassion kits are designed to help girls learn how to make jewelry so that they can start their own businesses and control their destinies through entrepreneurial spirit and financial independence.

Sharing History

Sixteen-year old documentarian Sydney Shavers made a movie about her great-great-great grandmother Elvira, who spent twenty-three years living as a slave in North Carolina. Sydney's brand signature involved illuminating the inspiring strength and resilience of her foremothers and forefathers. And, because a big part of Sydney's brand signature is sharing her appreciation for the heroic history of the African American people with future generations, she donated her film to the Richmond Black History Museum and Cultural Center of Virginia.

Brand Signatures That Include Fair Trade

The fair trade movement has expanded exponentially over the past few years. A project that began as a way to source products from responsible producers has grown into an extremely impactful organization worldwide.

✳ Words of Wisdom from Fairy Godparents ✳

"I work really hard at trying to see the big picture and not getting stuck in ego. I believe we're all put on this planet for a purpose, and we all have a different purpose . . . When you connect with that love and that compassion, that's when everything unfolds."

—Ellen DeGeneres, comedian, personality, philanthropist

What makes fair trade products different is that all the proceeds from fair trade–certified products are designated for social, economic, and environmental projects. In addition to supporting the growth of developing countries, fair trade producers also treat their workers fairly, meaning fair wages and fair working conditions. This idea of transparency that is present in many fair trade companies has become an integral part of many brand signatures. Beginning with simple everyday items like sugar, coffee, and bananas, the fair trade movement has expanded to include clothing, shoes, jewelry, furniture, and almost anything you may come into contact with in your daily life. Your business might use some of these materials—if so, you might want to consider using fair trade materials and incorporating that theme into your brand signature.

Larger brands like Patagonia, Hershey's Chocolate, and Honest Tea have all become fair trade–certified in an attempt to run a business that's conscious of how its materials are created. Patagonia's director of social and environmental responsibility says, "Offering Fair Trade products is an important new tool for us to help ensure fair wages and workplace safety for the workers in the supply chain who sew Patagonia clothes. We are also empowering the people purchasing our products." The fair trade movement is becoming increasingly important as awareness of environmental harms and social inequalities becomes more widespread. Using fair trade products might be important to you or your customers—if so, build it into your brand signature.

Brand Signatures That Include Profit with a Purpose

Many of today's most successful brands have made the idea of giving back a central part of their business vision. In this way, not only are they engaged in the enlightened business models of the future, and profiting with purpose, but allowing a cause or a mission to contribute to their brand signature.

Here are some examples of some of today's most innovative brands whose brand signature includes an element of giving back.

Warby Parker

★ The company (*www.warbyparker.com*) creates boutique-quality, classically crafted eyewear at a revolutionary price point with a quirky, relatable brand that works to create long-term relationships with customers.

★ This is "eyewear with a purpose." For every pair of glasses sold, the company gives a pair to someone in need. It partners with nonprofits such as Vision-Spring to train low-income entrepreneurs to sell affordable glasses. Since the company's inception in 2010, they have donated more than 500,000 pairs to communities in need. "We believe that everyone has the right to see."

★ Warby Parker serves the broader community in a variety of ways, including sponsoring a local Little League team and distributing glasses through its Buy a Pair, Give a Pair program.

- ★ Warby Parker is proud to be one of the few carbon-neutral eyewear brands in the world. The company tracks its greenhouse gas emissions at every step of its production and delivery processes and purchases mitigating carbon offsets.

- ★ Warby Parker's customer service philosophy is to "treat our customers the way we'd like to be treated." Their shopping innovations include the Virtual Try-On and Home Try-On features. They also create innovative consumer activation campaigns that take their online brand, offline, giving the consumers a chance to get a more "real" feel for the brand, literally and figuratively.

One World Futbol Project

- ★ One World's (*www.oneworldfutbol.com*) mission statement is: "We bring the healing power of play to youth worldwide by making, selling and distributing nearly indestructible balls that survive the harshest environments. Collaborating with sponsors, organizations and individuals, we deliver balls to disadvantaged communities where play and sport are used to foster social change."

- ★ The company has created a nearly indestructible ball that will last for years in any environment. It never goes flat, even if punctured. Similar to a soccer ball, it can be used for other games as well, and even comes in adult and youth sizes.

- ★ Buy One, Give One: For every One World Futbol purchased, the company donates one to an organization that supports disadvantaged communities. You can also donate balls directly to organizations in their network.

- ★ One World is taking the simple concept of play to make a change in the world. They feel that play helps heal and rebuild communities devastated by war, disaster, disease, and poverty.

- ★ Since their launch, One World and its partners have helped more than 15 million children and youth discover their heroic potential through play and the One World Futbol.

- ★ One World runs a variety of campaigns to match donors with communities in need. For example, in December 2013, One World teamed up with soccer player Landon Donovan and the LA Galaxy Foundation for the "Play It Forward" campaign. Targeting soccer fans, the program provided several ways for donors to contribute balls to One World's partner organizations.

TOMS Shoes

★ The most popular model of profit-for-purpose companies is the TOMS Shoes (*www.toms.com*) model of sell-one, give-one, meaning that for every pair of shoes they sell, they donate a pair to a child in need. Beginning in 2006, TOMS Shoes established their One for One model. TOMS started donating shoes to children in need in South America.

★ To date, TOMS has donated more than 10 million pairs of new shoes to children all over the world in more than sixty countries, partnering with organizations like IMA World Health and Save the Children.

★ Since 2011, TOMS has also worked to restore sight to the 285 million individuals living with sight issues. Using the same One for One model, TOMS helps restore the vision of one person, through glasses, sight-saving surgery, or medical treatment.

★ Most recently, TOMS has added a coffee company. For every bag of TOMS Roasting Company coffee sold, TOMS provides one week of clean water to an individual in need of it.

★ TOMS has not only begun to make a difference in the world, they have also garnered an impressive brand following through the strength of their brand signature. With more than 4 million followers on Twitter and Facebook, the TOMS brand is highly visible. This type of brand is the new norm, a socially driven brand that addresses the issues their customers are concerned about.

Nonprofit Brand Signatures

Erin Schrode and her organization Teens Turning Green are the perfect example of how one voice can inspire a world to change. Through grass-roots social media campaigns, speaking opportunities, and global action, Erin has gotten the word out and begun her crusade as the face of the new green generation.

In 2005, after working with The Schoolbag in Haiti for 5 years, Erin wanted to make a change within her own community and Teens Turning Green was born around her kitchen table in Mill Valley, California. Teens Turning Green's Project

Green Challenge launched in 2007, inviting college- and high-school-aged students around the country to participate in a month-long sustainability challenge. During its first year, Project Green Challenge had students from all 50 states participating, and it has now grown to engage over 2,700 students at 407 campuses, representing all 50 states and 30 countries.

⋆˙⋆ Words of Wisdom from Fairy Godparents ⋆˙⋆

"To any entrepreneur: if you want to do it, do it now. If you don't, you're going to regret it."

—Catherine Cook, cofounder of MyYearbook and MeetMe

Erin's voice is the change she wants to see in the world and it's getting noticed. Her brand signature is carried through everything Teens Turning Green does. She has recently been featured as a sustainability expert for the *New York Times*, *Vanity Fair*, *San Francisco Chronicle*, *Teen Vogue*, and *Huffington Post*. Her passion and vision inspire others to make a change and join her movement. Through digital campaigns and live speaking engagements, Erin and her world-changing initiatives are making a widespread impact.

Brand Signatures That Include Personality

Sometimes a brand signature is defined simply by a unique point of view. There are many brands today whose sole product is the interesting take that these Cinderella CEOs have on the world around them. Bloggers in the worlds of fashion, entertainment, and even the news are now able to have their voices heard around the world, and become brands in themselves that can spin off and support a number of products like books, television programs, YouTube channels, and even workshops and personal appearances—all based on a distinctive personality.

Tavi Gevinson, the Style Rookie

Teenage magazine publisher Tavi Gevinson first discovered her signature style when she realized that her fashion sense was a lot different from her friends'. For her, getting dressed in the morning wasn't just about looking pretty, but about expressing herself. She didn't like to go and hang out and shop at the mall to get a jump on the latest suburban trends like her other friends. Tavi loved to shop at thrift stores, to explore the world of vintage clothing, and to experiment with different looks that said something about who she was and what she was feeling on any particular day. Tavi was her own canvas for self-expression.

So as an outlet, Tavi started to blog on her dad's computer about her unique slant on fashion and life, and before she knew it, she had 50,000 readers a day visiting her blog, *www.thestylerookie.com*. And the numbers only increased exponentially from there. Soon, Tavi was being touted as the next fresh voice in fashion and her blogs were so subtly ironic and sophisticated that the media began to speculate that Tavi was actually an adult, not a teen at all!

Tavi took her rapid success in stride. She thought that she was just a passing trend, a flavor of the month that would disappear as quickly as legwarmers or fingerless gloves. So she didn't let herself get too excited and just kept on doing what she had always done, talking straight about what she saw and how she felt about it, and putting together some truly fantastic outfits to the surprise and sometimes dismay of her classmates, and the growing admiration of the world.

When the fashion designers and even the *New York Times* started calling to invite her to fashion week in New York City, Tavi began to realize that she was on to something that was maybe even bigger than a fashion blog. Tavi understood that she had a unique voice and perspective on life that people wanted to hear, especially other teen girls like her, who were different and perhaps just as confused and complicated as she was. So Tavi joined forces with her fairy godmother, Jane Pratt, former publisher of *Sassy* and *Jane*, and started a new magazine for girls, *Rookie*, dedicated to the idea of presenting teen girls as the complicated, sometimes contradictory, but always infinitely rich and interesting multidimensional people that they are. Today, *Rookie* has an editorial staff of fifty girls who all contribute their unique perspectives on the world. Rookiemag.com has published thirty-three issues as of May 2014, and Tavi has just published her first two books with a third on the way.

Embrace Personality in Your Brand Signature

Tavi Gevinson is a perfect example of the power you gain when you understand and accept yourself and put the gifts to work that only you can offer. Tavi built a teen empire based solely on the understanding of who she was, what she thought, and how she was different from—and the same as—other girls in the world. When you start to focus on and understand your personal take on things, you can begin to develop your voice and your talent, and reach out to others in a way you never thought possible. And once you do, you will be amazed at how many people out there will be lining up to listen to your truth.

◄ CINDERELLA CEO PROFILE ►

Tavi Gevinson
Rookie (style blog)
www.rookiemag.com

As Tavi said in an interview with BBC in 2012, "I think I surprise some people because a lot of the time I roll out of bed and go to school and I don't wear anything that interesting sometimes. But last year, technically at my school you're not allowed to wear a costume at Halloween because I guess people will die or something. But I did. But I got away with it because I think people just assumed that I was like wearing giant foam bunny ears because it was my outfit. Anna Wintour gave me those bunny ears. Of course I have to wear them.

"I went to fashion week for the first time when I was thirteen. People were confused about my being there for a few reasons; one was that I was a blogger. The word itself, 'blog,' it's kind of an ugly word. It just doesn't sound very legitimate. And fashion as an industry has been really behind about being online, so I think people were confused and angry that someone younger than them had figured it out. They would talk about how inappropriate it was for someone my age to be at fashion week. But this is coming from an industry that fetishizes youth!"

⁺✦ Chapter 1's Cinderella Principles ✦⁺

Indulge your curiosities: Develop your personal identity by trying everything you can!

Ask yourself questions: Pinpoint areas you are passionate about.

Realize that your path to success won't be straight: Venture off the beaten path, and don't be afraid to explore something different.

Turn cinders into silk: Work with what you have and turn your trouble spots into your best attributes.

Use your precious energy wisely: If you do, it'll turn a negative into a positive.

Build your foundation with a brand signature: Be consistent, be precise, and be yourself!

CHAPTER 2

Wish Out Loud

WRITE YOUR BUSINESS PLAN

So Cinderella went and shook the little tree, and said:

"Shake yourself, shake yourself, little tree. Throw some nice clothing down to me!"

She had scarcely spoken these words when a splendid silver dress fell down before her. With it were pearls, silk stockings with silver decorations, silver slippers, and everything else that she needed.

Planning for Fairy-Tale Success

Once Cinderella had identified the kind of future she wanted and deserved, she had to find the courage and clarity to express that view to the world. It wouldn't have done her any good to keep her vision to herself, counting lentils and merely dreaming of dancing at the ball. Cinderella had to manifest her wishes into the world by saying them out loud so that the forces of the universe could hear her. Further, she had to begin to live her newfound principles every day so that people who could make a difference would notice her gifts, and lend her a hand—or maybe a wave of a magic wand.

Cinderella begins quietly, content to go about her daily duties but letting her inner goodness shine through in everything she does, says, and thinks. She works hard, treats people (and animals) nicely, and sharpens her skills. Then, when she gains the courage, she says her wish out loud and suddenly a fairy godmother appears.

In today's business world, the most effective way to begin the process of declaring your wish to the world—and attracting the attention of fairy godmothers with the resources to make your wish a reality—is to write a business plan. A business plan is like a blueprint for your future. It details how you envision your wish opening up and flourishing in the world long-term. Your business plan shows that you have thoroughly considered your wish and how you'll make it happen. While a business plan might seem daunting and very official at first, Cinderella and her fairy godmother give us some very good tips and step-by-step instructions about how to put together all the elements that you will need to make your dream a reality.

Writing a Business Plan, Phase 1: Preparation

Approaching your business plan in little chunks is a good way to get it done without being overwhelmed. Give yourself a realistic timeline for getting the whole thing done, considering your other commitments—school, extracurriculars, job, etc. Assign deadlines for each phase to help keep yourself on track, and plan simple rewards for hitting them!

Step 1: Get Some Feedback

Make up a list of friends, family, neighbors, coworkers, classmates, and other contacts to ask for some feedback about your idea. Don't cheat yourself and stay comfortably within your inner circle. It's important to talk to old and trusted friends, but stretch yourself and include people on your list whom you don't know very well and who are of different ages from you so you get a fresh look at your idea from a variety of perspectives. Ask people for a little of their time, then run your idea by them. If some people are reluctant to help out, don't lose faith. Keep asking around until you get a good test market together.

When you are talking to people, don't ask questions as if you are a survey taker, but rather as if you are the owner or manager of the business, which you are—the business of you! Be friendly and appreciative with everyone you speak to and remember to listen more than you talk. You are there to learn, not to win them over to your way of thinking.

⁕ Words of Wisdom from Fairy Godparents ⁕

"It is our choices that show what we truly are, far more than our abilities."

—J.K. Rowling, author and billionaire

What you ask, and how you ask it, can go a long way toward determining the quality and quantity of the information you receive. Ask questions that are too specific and you run the risk of getting one-word answers that don't really give you the benefit of understanding what a person thinks. Ask questions that are too general and you wind up getting nonspecific information that isn't very useful to you.

Generally, it's a good idea to establish an open-minded and warm rapport with your subject, give them a little bit of information as to what you are looking for, and then ask questions that address the goals of your interview. Encourage your subject to expand on their answers—this, in turn, will give you lots of useful and specific information. For example, you could say:

"Thank you so much for agreeing to listen to my business idea. I'm thinking of starting a new jewelry line and I wanted to show you some of my initial pieces. What do you think? I worry about the cost of stones and my production time. Do you have any experience with this or know someone who does?"

Start the conversation with your "advisors" with interesting questions. The first couple of questions are critical to the success of the talk. Here are some generic examples of good questions that ensure an informative response.

1. What do you like the most about this product, service, idea?
2. What do you like the least about this idea?
3. If you add something to this idea, what would it be?
4. What would you tell a best friend or family member about this product, service, idea?
5. If you could only change one thing about this product, service, idea, what would you change, and what's the main reason that one thing needs changing?
6. If you were making a commercial for this product, what would the slogan be? What features would you emphasize?

Once you've gotten these answers, it's time to sift through them. Which ideas make sense to you? Do these suggestions align with where you see your brand going? These conversations are a jumping-off point; they are often the first time you're getting feedback on your ideas and that can be scary. Obviously, you don't have to make every change suggested to you, but if you hear yourself thinking "Oh, that makes sense," then maybe that is an idea you run with. Don't lose your own brand identity, but be open to suggestions and change.

Step 2: Create a Business Plan Support Group with Your Peers

It might sound odd, but creating a "business plan class" can build confidence and creativity, and also is a built-in sounding board, brain reserve, and source of support that you can reach out to when the going gets tough or you are at a loss for answers. To establish a rhythm and make steady, consistent progress, try to get together weekly or monthly and become a support group for finding your path and finding your future. Always remember that a group of people together is much stronger than one person. In the age of Skype, Google Hangout, and FaceTime, the network of peers you are creating doesn't have to be in your town or city.

If starting your own network seems too daunting, check out some of the organizations dedicated to providing valuable support to startup businesses. For example, New York–based company The Hatchery (*www.hatchery.vc*) connects startups with investors. It also hosts business pitching simulations, panel feedback, and a valuable network of individuals. There is no way to ensure that your idea won't be stolen during this type of collaborative session, but it pays to be open. Everyone is there for the same reason, so trust your peers.

Cinderella CEOs Who Started with a Class or Group

Each one of these teens took a business plan class in high school and wrote a business plan that led to a successful business venture before she had graduated from high school. Just goes to show you what a group of smart girls on a mission can do when they put their heads together!

Jessica Cervantes

> *"I fell in love with the idea of owning your own business."*
> —Jessica Cervantes

Jessica had loved experimenting with ingredients ever since her grandma taught her to bake. When she was only sixteen years old, she turned her passion into profit and developed her unique spin on the cupcake called PopsyCakes, which are cupcakes served on a pretzel stick. But it wasn't until Jessica became a part of the International Business and Finance Academy at John A. Ferguson Senior High school that baking and business came together in a brand-new recipe for success. Today, Jessica is the CEO of a growing business and has opened her very first PopsyCakes store in the Miami airport, right next to Starbucks and Häagen-Dazs!

Zoe Damacela

> *"Make an impression with everyone you meet and everything you do. You never know what it can lead to."*
> —Zoe Damacela

Zoe started making custom clothing for herself and her friends when she was just eleven years old. Realizing she was on to something, Zoe enrolled in a Network for Teaching Entrepreneurship class at her high school, learned how to write a business plan . . . and Zoe Damacela Apparel was born. Today, Zoe makes and sells her own designs online while attending Northwestern University on a full scholarship thanks to winning an entrepreneurial award. Zoe's entrepreneurial spirit extends beyond the scope of her own business ventures to youth and innovation across the nation. She attended Bill Clinton's Clinton Global Initiative in New York City and has been a keynote speaker for President Barack Obama's Startup America initiative.

Zermina Velic and Belma Ahmetovic

> *"If you have your mind set on doing something great, someone, somewhere, will realize it and lend you a helping hand."*
> —Belma Ahemtovic

These two Bosnian immigrants started their computer-repair service, Beta Bytes, for their community through a Network for Teaching Entrepreneurship program at their high school. Beta Bytes won first place in the Network For Teaching Entrepreneurship (NFTE) New England regional competition in 2010, the girls then moved on to compete in the NFTE National Youth Entrepreneurship Challenge. To be eligible to compete in this competition, Velic and Ahmetovic were required to develop and present an original business plan, learn real-world business expertise, and receive hands-on training in their field prior to the competition. Since their successful launch of Beta Bytes, the girls have moved on to do other things.

Zermina Velic attended Babson College and is now interning at an entrepreneurial nonprofit, Lemonade Day. Lemonade Day's tagline is "empowering today's youth to become tomorrow's entrepreneurs," which Velic has already achieved. She is working as their marketing, community engagement, and social media intern, driving engagement and awareness to the nonprofit while continuing to share her expertise with the world.

Belma Ahemtovic also attended Babson College, where she was the founder and CEO of an apparel company called Lazerwear Apparel and is now working at *The Hartford* as part of their Technology Development and Leadership Internship Program.

Shomari Patterson

"You have to be daring and willing to take risks, because sometimes the risks you take will be the best choices you have made for your business."
—Shomari Patterson

Shomari turned her passion for jewelry into a business when she was just fourteen years old. As socially aware as she is creative, Shomari wanted her jewelry company Shamazzle's Dazzles to contribute something to the world. With the $5,000 prize she received as second-place winner in the NFTE's National Youth Entrepreneurship Challenge of 2011, she plans to pursue a business major in college. Her ultimate goal is to take her company global and partner with nonprofits that empower girls.

Step 3: State Your Vision

Now that you have honed and tested your idea, the next step is to capture your vision on paper in a vision statement.

What are you creating? Make a rough outline of the specific vision you have for your business by writing down your answers to these questions.

1. What business are you creating exactly?
2. What will your business look like at startup?
3. What will your business look like in one year, three years, and five years?
4. What is your mission? Why are you starting this business?
5. What are your most important business goals?
6. How will you measure success?

Here is an example of our vision statement to guide you:

Our business is to write a book. We want to write and publish a book that raises awareness about the opportunities for young women to become entrepreneurs in today's economy. We want to create a platform for young entrepreneurs to connect and engage with each other both on- and offline around the subject of innovation, entrepreneurialism, and success. Our goal is to write the book, then find a publisher and then sell a lot of copies of the book. We would also like to write other books about this subject, and continue to keep our readership up-to-date on all of the recent trends and developments in this field. We will measure our success through numbers of copies sold and through the level of engagement on our social media pages.

_____

_____

_____

_____

_____

_____

_____

_____

Step 4: Figure Out How Your Company Is Different

It's really important to know why your business is different and better than each of your competitors'. Check out your competition closely. Where do you stand on price? Materials used? Delivery times? Style or approach? Chart out appropriate categories and highlight how your product or service is better than those around you.

Step 5: Define Your Business Strategy

Now let's address some of the specifics of your vision by writing down the answers to the following questions. This is how you create a business strategy that will take your idea up off the page and move it into the world of real business.

1. What exactly are you trying to achieve?
2. How exactly are you going to build your business? What is your first step?
3. What will your product or service be?
4. How is your idea or product different or better than your competition's? Is it a new niche within an established industry?

5. What is the budget you will need to get started?
6. How will you raise money?
7. What resources (materials, equipment) will you need to get started?
8. How will you get the word out?
9. Who else will need to be involved?
10. What do you anticipate your monthly income will be immediately after launch? In one year, three years, five years? It's hard to know these numbers for sure, but try to estimate based on the profit you will generate from sales minus your costs and project outward as best as you can. There will be time later, once you are actually in the field and making sales, to adjust your estimates.

These answers will help you determine the direction of your business as well as a general timeline to launch. These answers will be built upon in future sections, so remember them!

Writing a Business Plan, Phase 2: Writing Everything Out

Now that you have done some soul-searching and really thought through your idea, it's time to take all of that information and put it into a business plan format. This is the document that you will use to explain your wish to the world. Here is a step-by-step guide for creating this first and crucial road map to fairy-tale success.

Step 1: Write Your Introduction

An introduction should present the essence of your idea with pizzazz and passion, and state succinctly and clearly what you are doing and why. Strip the purpose and goal of your business down into the simplest terms possible by answering the following questions, then compile your answers into a narrative that will open your business plan with an unforgettable bang.

★ What is your idea?
★ What are you proposing to do with your idea?
★ What are your goals?

* ★ Why is your idea the greatest idea since sliced bread?
* ★ Why do you think you will be successful?
* ★ Why are you uniquely qualified to carry this wonderful new idea to the world?

Think of your introduction as your pitch piece. It's the written equivalent of a first impression—and you only get one chance to make one of those. So spend a lot of time working with your introduction, because if you don't get it exactly right from the top, you run the risk of people not reading further. This is the business equivalent of wishing out loud!

✦ Words of Wisdom from Fairy Godparents ✦

"Whatever you want in life, other people are going to want it too. Believe in yourself enough to accept the idea that you have an equal right to it."

—Diane Sawyer, journalist

The key is to be sure that anyone who reads the first paragraph will understand it—at least well enough to be able to ask the right questions. Don't include too much jargon, or make it too long and rambling. You wouldn't want a potential investor to toss aside your plan after the first paragraph because he or she couldn't understand what was being presented.

Here are some examples of successful introductory paragraphs:

> *Fashion sportswear company X is a new apparel store that caters to the Millennial community in Los Angeles. As our name suggests, our focus is to provide apparel and accessories and position ourselves as the top retail store servicing this particular market.*

We are the first and only Millennial-owned apparel store in Los Angeles. Our intentions are to obtain 80 percent market share and become a central hub of shopping activity.

Fashion sportswear company X has centralized itself directly in position to the Forever 21 locations and social activities of our target market. We believe that this is critical to our initial success and long-term growth.

Super Organic Pizza sells 10-inch-only pizzas to students living in and around the University of California in Santa Barbara. Orders are taken over the phone and via the web. Student employees use their own bikes to deliver orders. An app has been created for use on campus as well for "quick" orders where you receive your pizza within twenty minutes of ordering.

Primary Goals:

★ Sell a healthier food option (organic pizza!) to students on campus
★ Simplify the ordering process
★ Highlight the carbon footprint reduction of using people on bikes to deliver pizza rather than cars.

Step 2: Spell Out Your Marketing Strategy

In this section of your business plan, you should discuss who you think your target market is and how you intend to reach out to them with your idea. Details in this section should include market demographics, which talk about how large your target market is as well as where they live, how old they are, where they shop, where they look for new ideas, and how you intend to put yourself in those places.

Are there places where you can speak, post online, or set up a booth that puts you right at the heart of your target market so that you can build awareness? Do your research and brainstorm all kinds of creative ways to reach out to your market and engage them on a regular basis, so that they will become loyal customers and ambassadors for your brand. Write all of your great ideas down in this section.

Here is an example of a successful marketing section. One of our favorite startup brands—AWAKE Chocolate out of Canada (*www.awakechocolate.com*)—was founded by Matt Schnarr, Dan Tzotzis, and Adam Deremo right after college. They shared the marketing section of their business plan with us:

> *Marketing Objective for AWAKE Chocolate*
> ★ Become the "go to" product for a great-tasting way to wake up
> ★ Establish higher usage rate than chocolate bars (caffeine + chocolate)
> ★ Hit higher penetration rates than energy drinks—>10 percent household penetration
>
> *To achieve those objectives, we will:*
> ★ Develop a lifestyle brand with major buzz that people want to try AWAKE and talk about the product
> ★ Be visible whenever people are looking for great taste or a pick me up
> ★ Anchor AWAKE around occasions and function to promote ritualized consumption
> ★ Get product into as many mouths as possible to demonstrate taste and efficacy
> ★ Partner with fraternities and sororities to seed chocolate around Greek Life

Step 3: Create a Budget

Numbers are where the rubber meets the road in terms of the viability of your idea, so do your research and Google everything you can think of in order to figure out how much things cost. The goal here is to come up with a realistic budget that will support your new business venture long enough for it to be successful. You need to provide real numbers that potential investors can evaluate when considering backing your great endeavor!

Here is an example of a successful budget outline to help get you started on your own.

Category	Budget Amount
INCOME	
Sales Revenue	
Interest Income	
Investment Income	
Other Income	
Total Income	
EXPENSES	
Accounting/Bookkeeping	
Marketing/Advertising	
Bank Service Charges	
Estimated Taxes	
Health Insurance	
Hiring Costs	
Inventory Purchases	
Legal Expenses	
Licenses/Permits	
Loan Payments	
Website/Blog Fees	
Payroll	
Printing/ Design	
Rent/Lease Payments	
Subscriptions and Dues	
Utilities and Telephone	
Vehicle Expenses	
Other	
Total Expenses	
TOTAL INCOME MINUS TOTAL EXPENSES	

Here is a simplified budget outline to guide you in creating your own.

SAMPLE BUDGET FORECAST FOR ONE YEAR					
	Forecasted 1st Qtr (Jan–Mar)	Forecasted 2nd Qtr (Apr–June)	Forecasted 3rd Qtr (July–Sept)	Forecasted 4th Qtr (Oct–Dec)	Totals
Revenues from product or service	$920,500	$978,000	$698,500	$627,750	$3,224,750
Cost to provide/ make profit or service	857,500	906,750	643,750	576,250	2,984,250
Gross Profit	*63,000*	*71,250*	*54,750*	*51,500*	*240,500*
Operating Expenses					
Advertising	1,500	1,500	1,500	1,500	6,000
Bank Charges	340	340	340	340	1,360
Dues and Subscriptions	1,475	1,475	1,475	1,475	5,900
Employee/ Client Relations	333	333	333	333	1,332
Legal and Accounting	3,642	3,642	3,642	3,642	14,568
Miscellaneous	589	589	589	589	2,356
Office Expense	8,863	8,863	8,863	8,863	35,452
Rent	2,058	2,058	2,058	2,058	8,232
Salaries	25,000	25,000	25,000	25,000	100,000
Taxes and Licenses	-	-	-	-	-
Telephone/ Internet	1,727	1,727	1,727	1,727	6,908

Total Operating Expenses	48,367	48,367	48,367	48,367	193,468
Income (Gross Profit – Operating Expenses)	**14,633**	**22,883**	**6,383**	**3,133**	**47,032**

It's most important to try and estimate your profits and losses as accurately as you can, but don't expect your numbers to be exact. Do your research, set your pricing, consider your production costs, estimate how many sales you think you can realistically make in one year. Then try to give some thought as to how you think you might be able to grow and expand through your second year, and your third. Don't be worried about not making a huge profit your first year. If you break even, this is perfectly fine. Just make sure that you have plans in place to expand your growth and generate profit over a three-year period.

⋆⋆ Words of Wisdom from Fairy Godparents ⋆⋆

"You only live once, but if you do it right, once is enough."

—Mae West, actress and singer

Step 4: Write Your Conclusion

Your business plan should conclude with a reiteration of the mission and goals you articulated in your introductory paragraph. It should draw everything together into a powerful and meaningful crescendo that really sells your whole idea and projects your ultimate future entrepreneurial awesomeness and success.

Now What Do You Do?

Your business plan is your foot in the door with investors. For others to see your business as a serious venture, this business plan needs to be rock solid. It also needs to be clearly understandable to people outside of your company, as you will be taking this to investors and venture capitalists. This plan will be the road map for your entire business!

Chapter 2's Cinderella Principles

Plan for fairy-tale success:
Envision your plan in the long-term.

Prepare your business plan:
Approach it in chunks, give yourself a realistic timeline, and keep yourself on track.

Collect information: Get feedback from everyone, ask questions, and keep an open mind.

Form a business plan support group: Work on your idea with others in a collaborative environment.

State your vision: Outline your idea and state your goals.

Define your business strategy: Outline action steps to achieve your goals.

Write out your business plan:

Write your introduction: Simplify your goals and purpose.

Spell out your marketing strategy: Detail your target audience and how to reach them.

Create a budget: Be as realistic as possible.

Write your conclusion: Reiterate your missions and goals and tie everything together.

CHAPTER 3

Make Practical Magic

★

GET FUNDING

This godmother of hers, who was a fairy, said to her, "You wish that you could go to the ball; is it not so?" "Yes," cried Cinderella, with a great sigh. "Well," said her godmother, "be but a good girl, and I will contrive that you shall go." Then she took her into her chamber, and said to her, "Run into the garden, and bring me a pumpkin."

Cinderella went immediately to gather the finest she could get, and brought it to her godmother, not being able to imagine how this pumpkin could help her go to the ball. Her godmother scooped out all the inside of it, leaving nothing but the rind. Having done this, she struck the pumpkin with her wand, and it was instantly turned into a fine coach, gilded all over with gold.

You Might Already Have a Lot of What You Need

One of the most important lessons that Cinderella's fairy godmother teaches her is that she already has most of what she will need to take her to the ball, as long as she learns how to make the most of what she has on hand. Cinderella's fairy godmother turns a pumpkin into a carriage simply by scooping out the seeds, and six white mice become finely dressed footmen with a wave of her magic wand. In other words, she shows Cinderella that with just a little innovation and imagination, you can make practical magic with the resources that you have lying around once you learn to see and reveal the hidden value in ordinary things.

When Adele Taylor was thirteen, she noticed that some of her peers struggled with reading and realized that many people have little access to books. Yet she and a lot of people she knew had plenty of books lying around. So she launched a book donation program. Today, Adele's Literacy Library gives everyone, regardless of age, access to the books they need to achieve literacy. Adele's company is a perfect example of how you can create an empire out of the resources you have right on hand. Since 2008, her group has distributed more than 5,000 books in Monroe Township, New Jersey.

How to Find Outside Funding

Try as you might to use your own resources, you'll probably come to a point where you need funding of some kind. Today, there are lots of options to gain extra funds, ranging from crowdfunding websites to partnering with an investor. This chapter will outline all you need to know to find the money your business deserves.

Crowdfunding

Crowdfunding takes it name from the fact that your project is funded by a large group of individuals using their own personal funds. To start with, you propose the idea that you wish to see funded. People interested in your idea can then choose how much money they want to give you. The power of crowdfunding is undeniable.

Gone are the days when small businesses are doomed to fail. This is a great option to consider when trying to raise money.

These crowdfunding sites all have a built-in application to deal with payments. Sites like Kickstarter, Fundable, or Indiegogo provide the perfect way for businesses to locate funds for a new startup. Crowdfunding has exploded in popularity, getting attention from both investors and businesses. It has received praise in the media, making the crowdfunding option a more legitimate way to raise extra funds. Many influential companies and individuals have used crowdfunding websites to raise money for their personal projects. Often, if a project is doing exceptionally well, the media will pick it up and tell its story, which, sometimes, turns into interest from a larger investor.

This is a great new tool for startups that has really caught on; however, this popularity also means an increase in competition. So if you choose this route, make sure that your campaign is a compelling one that stands out and speaks to your target market, and works effectively within the parameters of the funding site. These websites often use social algorithms to decide which projects should be promoted to the front page and be covered in the blog. Since there are so many projects out there looking for funding, getting lots of social-media support is key to avoid being lost in the clutter. The projects with more social interaction get promoted to the front page, so the more your project is shared the more eyeballs your page will get. In order to make your campaign compelling, you have to have the complete package: create some original content in the form of video and photos and make sure your brand messaging is clear. You want this audience to understand your product and realize that this is something they would like to use. Let's take a look at the three biggest players out there.

Kickstarter

Kickstarter (*www.kickstarter.com*) has become somewhat of a soapbox for creators to take their passion from a dream to a reality. By combining social media with real-life ideas, creators are able to take donations and turn their very own fairy tale into reality. Kickstarter has grown to garner support from organizations like TED and the Rhode Island School of Design, who are hand-selecting projects they would like to see funded. Kickstarter is not only a place to raise money for a conceptual idea; it has also become a place to share ideas and start a movement.

Debbie Sterling had an idea; she wanted to create a toy that would encourage girls to pursue careers in engineering. As a Stanford engineer herself, Debbie wanted to create something that would foster an interest in science and engineering in girls the way LEGO products and Erector sets had been inspiring boys for over 100 years. Debbie took her idea to Kickstarter, along with a catchy YouTube video, and secured over twice what her original funding goal had been. Less than one year later, GoldieBlox is sold in over 1,000 stores nationwide, including Toys "R" Us, and Debbie's "more than a princess" message has been featured in *USA Today*, *Huffington Post*, *Forbes*, *The Wall Street Journal*, and many more.

·*· Words of Wisdom from Fairy Godparents ·*·

"I believe in pink. I believe that laughing is the best calorie burner. I believe in kissing, kissing a lot. I believe in being strong when everything seems to be going wrong. I believe that happy girls are the prettiest girls. I believe that tomorrow is another day and I believe in miracles."

—Audrey Hepburn, actress

Kickstarter serves as more than an outlet to raise money; it has also become a place to share ideas and make a change. In 2012, 10 percent of the films at Sundance Film Festival were Kickstarter projects; a Kickstarter-funded book, *FUBAR*, made the *New York Times* bestseller list, and two Kickstarter-funded films, *Kings Point* and *Inocente*, were nominated for Oscars. The future of crowdfunding looks bright as Kickstarter-funded products continue to hit the market in 2014.

Indiegogo

Indiegogo (*www.indiegogo.com*) began in 2008 as a way for individuals to take their passion projects to the next level. Their mission is "to get your passion funded." What makes Indiegogo different from many other crowdfunding companies is their social integration. Where Kickstarter obviously offers a way to share your project online, Indiegogo has seamlessly integrated this into their software. Whether you're tech savvy or not, all it takes is one click to get the word out via social media or e-mail.

Indiegogo also rewards outreach. Through their own algorithm, called a project's "gogofactor," they reward individuals who are doing more outreach, sharing more, and, ultimately, raising more money by promoting these projects further on their own social channels and/or featuring them on the homepage of the Indiegogo website. This secures even further reach and visibility.

They also offer a unique support system of experts that are available around the clock to help entrepreneurs succeed with their projects. All of their support is personalized to each project, so they ensure that you are actually getting the help you need from others who know what they're doing.

In addition, Indiegogo offers an international projects section, which many other crowdfunding sites do not. Indiegogo, therefore, has become more of a place for cause-related fundraising and less about physical goods (the goods are still there, but there is often a cause backing them).

In the past year Indiegogo has begun to see celebrity clientele, including James Franco and Lil Wayne. Why would any of these people need to use Indiegogo, you ask? All of these stars were looking to raise awareness for a different charity.

★ The famous man of many hats, James Franco, used Indiegogo to fund his film project. He wanted to turn three of his short stories into three separate feature films. He has chosen to donate all proceeds from his films to a nonprofit called The Art of Elysium, which encourages actors, artists, and musicians to donate their time to children struggling with serious medical conditions. Although Franco did not reach his goal, he raised enough to put the films into production while raising a lot of awareness about a previously unknown good cause.

★ Rapper Lil Wayne wanted to give back to his roots. After growing up in the low-income neighborhood of Hollygrove, New Orleans, he wanted to give other high-risk youth around the country access to after-school programs. He partnered with The Motivational Edge, a nonprofit outreach program serving inner-city youth with a focus on music and art. They were active in Miami and South Beach; with Wayne's help, they were able to raise over $60,000 to expand to Phoenix, Arizona, where they were able to serve another 400 inner-city students.

★ You don't have to be an A-list celebrity to benefit from Indiegogo. New York City–based photographer Brandon Stanton, widely known for his photo campaign Humans of New York, has been a part of multiple Indiegogo campaigns since November 2012. Every one of his campaigns has well surpassed its funding goal. His most successful campaign to date was in partnership with Tumblr, working to raise money for victims of Hurricane Sandy. Originally looking to reach a goal of $100,000, Brandon was able to more than double that amount in just eleven days, raising $318,530 for Hurricane Sandy relief.

Fundable

Fundable (*www.fundable.com*) is a crowdfunding site for startups that helps entrepreneurs gain backers and raise capital. Fundable followed the passage of the JOBS Act (or "Crowdfunding Act"), which allows companies to publicly raise money from anyone willing to back them.

Fundable is selective about the companies that they work with. They are only interested in businesses that are very serious and very motivated. Fundable asks the startups they choose to create a company profile that provides an overview of the company, its product, and its funding goals. Fundable then helps startups choose rewards or equity and set their fundraising terms. Additionally, they help market startups' fundraising efforts, and assist them in gathering backers and collecting funds. Popular companies on Fundable include Bia Sport, a wearable technology company; Sky Springs, a sustainable water company; and TuneGo, a music discovery network.

Fundable contributed to the success of Bia, a multisport GPS watch, made for women, by women. In just forty days of working with Fundable, Bia elicited the support of 2,118 backers, and surpassed its goal by bringing in $408,160, proving that the sleek watches for female athletes were in high demand. Additionally, pre-sales to date exceed 2,500 units, or $550,000.

Working with an Investor

Another way to gather what you need to take your dream up off the page is to find a fairy godmother who not only wants to mentor you, but is willing to put her money where her mouth is.

Before You Start Searching

The first thing to remember when approaching investors is that they will expect you to be prepared. You are asking them to invest their own money in your idea, so how can you show them that your idea will succeed as you anticipate? If the following things are not prepared, wait to meet with investors until they are.

Ask yourself these questions before meeting with an investor:

1. Do you know exactly how much money you are asking for?
2. Do you have a good business plan?
3. Do you have your pitch and brand messaging down?
4. Who will be a part of your team?
5. Do you have an appropriate outfit?
6. How will you get to the meeting?
7. Have you created your presentation and printed hard copies for those attending the meeting?

After the meeting, remember to follow up and provide the investor with an electronic copy of your business plan, presentation, and any supplementary documents she may have asked for.

Venture Capitalists

Not surprisingly, venture capitalists seldom provide startup funding to risky entrepreneurial ventures. Because venture capitalists don't typically work with entrepreneurs, you'll have a lot of obstacles to overcome to attract their attention. Here are some factors venture capitalists look for.

A VC's Checklist

★ **A unique idea that warrants a trademark or patent:** What are you offering that's different from your competitors or what is already on the market? This should be one of the first things you tell potential investors. In a May 2013 interview with Mashable, Charley Polachi, partner at Polachi Access Executive Search, stated, "Venture capitalists are looking to fund projects that are unique and can't be easily replicated. Ideally, the technology or service can be patented or trademarked to give the startup some breathing room and really allow the business some time to gain traction and marketshare."

★ **An airtight sense of what sets you apart:** Venture capitalists know the market. Many have been in the business for upwards of twenty years, so they have seen it all. Your business plan and overall strategy need to show why you're different. You did a lot of this research back when you created your business plan.

★ **Customers in hand:** Early-stage VCs want to see that they will be making a return on their investment. If you don't have a proven sample market, this becomes difficult for them to see. Make sure you have done some beta testing and are able to show them that your company is one that consumers respond positively to, preferably with some monetary gain.

★ **The Dream Team:** Often, startup companies don't get the product or the market right on the first time, and a VC might fall in love with your spirit (please notice the word *might*) and this is where your team comes in. This doesn't need to be a team of graphic designers, analysts, and business execs. As long as your team has complementary skills to yours, you are on your way to a good team. Since you are likely working alone at this point, you may have a hard time catching the attention of the VCs. If so, it might be time to find one or two team members with experience to support you through this process. The power of many minds is greater than the power of one!

Where to Find Venture Capital

Ask yourself what kind of investor works best for your business or movement. Do you want a small business investor, a venture capital firm, an angel investor, an equity investor, or something totally different? It's important to decide whom you will be targeting so you are able to tailor your business plan, and so you choose the right relationship that works for you and your company. Here's a quick rundown of the types of investors you can work with and why they might be right for your company.

- ★ **Small business investor:** A small business investor will give you a smaller amount of money for a set purpose; for example, buying new equipment. The good thing about small business investors is that they don't give you a set schedule to return their investment, so you are able to repay when you have secured your own funds.
- ★ **Venture capitalist firm:** A venture capitalist firm provides financial aid to early-stage, high-potential, high-risk startup companies. The venture capitalist firm owns equity in your company, meaning that they own a part of your company until the loan is repaid. They often command control over company decisions and a large part of the company ownership.
- ★ **Angel investors:** An angel investor is an affluent individual who provides capital for a startup in exchange for debt or equity. These individuals are often part of a larger group of angel investors that works together to fund startup companies.
- ★ **Equity investors:** An equity investor receives shares of your company stock in exchange for financial assistance. These investors become a part of the company until they choose to sell their shares in the company to another investor.

Once you have figured out which type of funding might work for you, then you can start scouting potential funders. Start your search by reaching out to your circle of experts, friends, family, and associates, and begin to gather ideas for people that might be interested in investing in your idea. You can also begin to search and approach investment companies that have an interest in funding projects like yours.

Investment Companies

Here are a couple of our favorite investment companies to give you an idea of the possibilities that are out there.

Golden Seeds

Golden Seeds (*www.goldenseeds.com*) is an early-stage investment firm with a focus on women leaders in business. Golden Seeds, however, is neither a venture capital firm nor an angel network; it's both. Their venture capital program currently boasts three different funds investing in more than thirty-five companies, and their angel network is composed of over 275 members in New York, Boston, Silicon Valley, and Texas.

Currently, Golden Seeds' portfolio is made up of female-centric brands ranging from fashion to education and everywhere in between. Like every major venture capitalist firm or angel investor, Golden Seeds has strict criteria for whom and what they choose to invest in, but the two major questions they consider when evaluating women entrepreneurs are:

1. Does she have power and influence in the company?
2. Is she the majority owner of the company?

At this point, you may be the only owner (and employee) of your company, so the answer to these questions should be yes!

Investors' Circle

Investors' Circle (*www.investorscircle.net*) is the self-proclaimed "oldest, largest and most successful early-stage impact-investing network." Investors' Circle focuses on brands and companies that are making an impact on the world, particularly in social, environmental, health, and education matters. Since IC's founding in 1992, it has invested $166 million in the projects of 265 companies, and since 2012 it has increased its investments by 400 percent. If your business's brand signature includes key components that match Investors' Circle's, consider contacting them for funding.

Angel Investors

Angel investors are different from VCs in the sense that they are individuals, not companies or groups. They are willing to invest in high-risk startups and often know that they are going to lose their investment during a company's first round of funding. That's why they require a very high return on their investments. They take equity in your company and will become an involved member of your board. Some of the world's largest businesses, including Google and Facebook, have received angel investing.

Angel investors will be more involved in your company than venture capitalists because they have invested their own personal funds. Many times, an angel investor will also become somewhat of an advisor to your company. There is a strong emphasis on personal relationships between entrepreneurs and angel investors because often they are working closely together. Your angel investor must be the right fit for your company, because you will most probably be working closely together on making your business a success. Because angel investors are investing not only in a company but also in the people involved in that company, personalities count.

When approaching this kind of an investor, do your due diligence on your own company because you will be asked the hard questions about what the future looks like and your investor will expect you to have answers. You've already done a lot of thinking about this when you created your business plan, but expect angel investors to try to find holes in your thought process or to point out faulty logic. Their job is to vet businesses like yours, so this is second nature to them.

Finding Angel Investors

The best angel for you is going to be a local, high-net individual. They like to be hands-on with their investments, meaning they need to be close by in location. There are also multiple resources that match investors with startups. You can create a profile on a website like AngelList (*www.angel.co*) that allows startups and businesses to post what they need and creates a database for investors to find them.

With unprecedented access to investor databases and Google searches, it has become much simpler to find potential angel investors. Here are some of our favorite angel investment resources to get you started.

★ Angelsoft (*www.angelsoft.net*): Almost every other angel network that matches investors with startup companies in their area uses Angelsoft's software.

★ Keiretsu Forum (*www.keiretsuforum.com*): This one claims to be "the world's largest angel investor network, with 850 accredited investor members."

★ Angel Capital Association (ACA) (*www.angelcapitalassociation.org*): Comprised of multiple Angel groups, this is the largest Angel association in Northern America.

Royal Role Model Q&A

Clara Tate

Tell us a little about your background.

I began my fairy-tale training while studying abroad at Trinity University in Dublin, Ireland. As a psychology and anthropology double major at Mount Holyoke College, I went to Trinity wanting to pursue my already determined majors but also to explore classes such as English, journalism, and Irish history. I realized my ideal job would be one where I could combine my passions of writing, psych, and anthro, and so I decided to find an internship in the field of public relations. That summer I interned with Stearns Johnson Communications, a boutique PR firm in San Francisco specializing in consumer tech products. I felt passionate about the startups I was working with, and even more passionate about forming relationships with media in the hopes of securing placements for my clients in top-tier publications.

After graduating from Mount Holyoke in 2013, I interned with FleishmanHillard for eight months, specializing in media relations and social media strategy for clients including healthcare, consumer, corporate, and tech. I recently joined the team at Arieff Communications as an Account Coordinator.

Do you have any words of wisdom for other young women?

Don't waste time being unhappy. Surround yourself with people who lift you up, not bring you down. Find friends who make you a better person, who make you smile, laugh, and who encourage you to take risks and fight for what you want.

What's the best tip you've received on success?

Be selfish. Make decisions that will drive your career forward, not hold you back. In the end, a company is a company, and it can always find someone to replace you. You owe it to yourself to take the necessary measures to further your career, even if that means leaving your first job, a company you may feel loyal and indebted to for all you learned from them.

Do you have advice on starting your career?

I am not entitled to have a job. Someone took a chance when deciding to hire me, based on a few references and my resume. I am not in the clear now that I have been hired, but rather am blessed with the opportunity to prove myself to this company and do the best that I can do.

What are your guilty pleasures?

Horses. Whether I'm riding, mucking out stalls, or cleaning tack, I am the happiest when I'm surrounded by horses. I would drop just about anything to be around horses every day, to smell like hay and saddle soap, like I was in college.

How have your parents helped you achieve success?

My parents have given me unconditional love and support. They encouraged me to go to a college where I not only received a great education, but was able to follow my passion for equestrian. Knowing that I can always count on them for guidance, advice, a home cooked meal every now and then, and just a hug when I'm feeling down is the greatest feeling.

Is it scary to follow your heart?

Following your heart often means leaving behind what is most comfortable to you. Any change is scary, and leaving behind someone or something that has been a constant in your life for something uncertain would make anyone uneasy. But it is leaving our comfort zone and taking those risks that move us forward. Taking a leap of faith and following your heart will never being a regret. It's waiting around hoping for something to happen rather than making it happen that will be your greatest regret.

Keeping It in the Family

Your family wants to see you succeed and may even want a stake in your business idea and future success! There are many ways your family can lend resources to your startup business. Given her lack of family support, Cinderella had to rely on her animal friends since her family treated her horribly. You might be in a better situation with your family! If so, consider adding them to your business team.

Funding

Your family might be one of the first places you think of to provide some funding. If anyone wants to contribute, you need to treat the situation professionally and responsibly. Even though you are dealing with family members, make sure to keep business matters professional, not personal, and write up a contract so no feelings get hurt. Outline what each party's expectations are, including specifics for how and when the money will be paid back. Look for resources online to help you draw up a contract, such as LegalZoom (*www.legalzoom.com*). Have a lawyer review your contract so everything is clearly spelled out and there are no misunderstandings. Many great businesses were started based on parents helping their kids financially—for example, Method founders Adam Lowry and Eric Ryan borrowed money from their parents to help get their green cleaning company off the ground. The key is to establish a clear and mutually understood arrangement that you both respect.

Family as Business Partners

Family members can also make for great business partners. A mom, for example, can be a great business partner as long as serious boundaries are established at the beginning.

You need to make sure they understand that this is your project and leave control of the company to you.

Do:

★ Ask for their opinion
★ Use their business expertise
★ Use them as your test subjects

Don't:

★ Accept monetary help from them unless it's outlined in a contract
★ Allow them to take control of the company

Successful Mother-Daughter Teams

One of our favorite mother-daughter businesses is the writing duo P.J. and Traci Lambrecht, who are a bestselling book team. Some of their novels include *Live Bait*, *Dead Run*, *Snow Blind*, and *Shoot to Thrill*, all of which are bestsellers. Another great mom-daughter team founded StyleLikeU (*www.stylelikeu.com*). StyleLikeU was founded in 2009 by Lily Mandelbaum and her mother Elisa Goodkind as a multimedia outlet that highlighted individuals with unique style stories. Through profiles, webisodes, daily posts, and lots of style inspiration, Lily and Elisa have created a massive style network that is unlike many others. They wanted to challenge the unattainable idea that you needed to be "on trend" or "beautiful" to be a part of the fashion world.

These women are rethinking fashion by taking it off the runway and into real life. According to their website, they wrote that fashion "embod[ies] a culture where people are honored for their differences and connected through personal, universal truths." What they have accomplished is a beautiful expression of authenticity in fashion through this project that has been extremely successful.

During the '80s and '90s, Elisa was a Fashion Stylist and Editor for numerous top fashion magazines, including *Vanity Fair*, *Interview*, *InStyle*, *Glamour*, and *Self.* After taking a break from her passion for the art of fashion to raise her children and to teach yoga, Elisa returned to the industry. Lily, having grown up as a curvy girl surrounded by her mom's eclectic and free-spirited friends, was more intrigued by them than by the Photoshopped fashion magazine spreads featuring hipless models whose trendy clothes left her feeling ill-at-ease about her more voluptuous physique.

After seeing each other's struggles within the confines of the current fashion landscape, one day Elisa and Lily, both sharing a passion for those who expressed themselves consciously through clothing, decided to pick up their home-video camera and begin documenting the individuals who genuinely inspired them. Since then, the duo has interviewed more than 800 empowering individuals, each of whom prove that style cannot be bought.

Sister Acts

Siblings can also make great business partners. One example is a brother-sister team—Brienne Ghafourifar, eighteen, and cofounder/brother Alston, twenty, who started Entefy (*www.entefy.com*), about which their site states: "Entefy brings together your e-mail, text, voice, video, and social conversations so you can connect with people, not apps." They used the tagline "Better Together" to tie their relationship into their business.

Brienne and her team closed on funding commitments from private angels of $1 million (the youngest college graduate to raise this kind of money). While reading about this girl you realize that she (a) had the support of her parents, (b) had the commitment to her startup, and (c) would not take no for an answer. These are skills you need for fundraising. Be persistent, and keep on moving forward.

A Father-Daughter Business

Vivienne Harr started with a lemonade stand . . . and she is now the proud owner of Make A Stand, a lemonade company, and the Make A Stand Foundation, working to eradicate child slavery. This eight-year-old saw something bigger than herself after visiting a museum with her father and seeing photos of enslaved Nepalese children. She asked patrons to her lemonade stand to donate "whatever was in their heart" and after about six months, ended up donating $101,320 to Not For Sale (*www.notforsalecampaign.org*). Today, Vivienne has published a children's book, *When Life Gives You Lemons, Change the World!*, explaining the message that big things start small and "you don't have to be big or powerful to change the world. You can be just like me!" She is also releasing a documentary film, *Stand with Me*, about her journey to raise awareness about child slavery around the world, and also spread the message that you too can do something to make a change.

Make A Stand lemonade is organic and fair trade, available in 137 stores and is expected to gross $2 million in 2015, 5 percent of which will be donated to hand-selected organizations that are doing leading work in eradicating child slavery around the world. Make A Stand has also made donations to other organizations, including Free the Slaves (*www.freetheslaves.net*), Nepal Youth Foundation (*www .nepalyouthfoundation.net*), and GEMS: Girls Educational & Mentoring Services (*www.gems-girls.org*).

Win Money in a Contest

Perhaps another sign of the growing support of small business startups is the number of contests that encourage innovation by offering a large financial reward. MIT offers rewards of more than $350,000 each year for its pitch, accelerate, and launch contests.

To improve your odds of success in these contests, find ways to make your project stand out in the crowd. You'll have to either present your idea in person or pitch it through an essay, so the idea itself has to be as original as possible.

Example: Duck Tape held a contest challenging young designers to create prom-night fashion using Duck Tape, inspired by the Stuck at Prom Scholarship Contest. Then students submitted their Duck Tape looks and the winner won a scholarship.

Following is a list of famous contests that might fit your venture:

★ **The NYU Stern New Venture Competition:** *www.stern.nyu.edu/experience-stern/about/departments-centers-initiatives/centers-of-research/berkley-center/programs/venture-competitions/about/*
★ **Student Entrepreneur National Competition:** *www.enactus.ca/what-we-do/student-entrepreneurs/student-entrepreneur-national-competition/*
★ **BDC Young Entrepreneur Award contest:** *www.bdcyoungentrepreneuraward.ca/en/home*
★ **National Youth Entrepreneurship Challenge:** *www.nfte.com/what/national-challenge*

- ★ **The Global Student Entrepreneur Awards:** *www.gsea.org*
- ★ **MIT $100K Entrepreneurship Competition:** *www.mit100k.org*
- ★ **Annual Amazing Entrepreneur Business Plan Competition:** *www.amazing entrepreneurcontest.com*

Building a Business on a Budget

Getting your business off the ground can cost a lot more than you expected. There are plenty of ways to save money, however. The following tips can help you put that valuable funding you've received directly into your product or service, not into all the other logistics of a startup.

Start at Home

Instead of paying to rent business space, consider the economic benefits of starting your business at home. Start working at home or in a shared office space with other small businesses. (Check WeWork, *www.wework.com*, or Google "shared work spaces" in your region.) It may not be the ideal way to start, but it will allow you to get off the ground on a shoestring budget.

If you need or want to start your small business in a retail space, every dollar saved will help you survive the lean first months! Here are some pros and cons to help you decide whether you need to rent a space or not.

Pros of an office space:
- ★ Place to see clients
- ★ Your own space for your company
- ★ Another way to get your brand message across
- ★ Quiet place to work

Cons:
- ★ Expensive!
- ★ Unnecessary until you have a team

Create a Co-op

Consider building partnerships with other business providers. There may be a number of products or services that are compatible with your own, and a partnership can be a mutually beneficial way of attracting new customers. We love Etsy as a great platform for e-commerce. Through Etsy, small producers are able to showcase their products to a large audience through a trusted third-party site. This is the case with Pinterest as well. Many clothing companies, like Nordstrom, have started uploading all new products to Pinterest first, allowing their followers to exclusively shop the collection before it is available anywhere else.

Buy Used

You don't have to buy everything new. You can save big money by buying the majority of the equipment for your business used. Though it may not be the dream way you want to start your business, it is the smart financial move. Check Craigslist or eBay for used conference consoles (those complicated-looking conference call speakers), keyboards, furniture, and other large items. You should invest in new computers and things to make your office your own!

Buy in Bulk

When it comes to the business supplies that you have to buy new, remember that it pays to buy in bulk. If you know you are going to need it and it is something that does not age, then buy as much as you can afford to as a way to keep your costs as low as possible. There are many office storage solutions, from IKEA cubbies to stackable boxes, to house your bulk supplies.

Advertise for Free

Don't waste money paying for advertising when you're just getting off the ground. With the advent of social media, it is now possible to completely advertise your business online for free. We discuss a lot of social media strategies in Chapter 5—remember, the vast majority of those are free! Mine those opportunities rather than paying for advertising.

Beyond social media, always be ready to advertise your brand. Carry business cards with your contact details and your website address. Include links to your website and blog (if you have one) within your e-mail signature. Use headed paper, complete with the same details, when writing to customers and suppliers. You needn't spend a lot of money on these things, but keep the design clean, professional, and consistent. Check TinyPrints (*www.tinyprints.com*), Vistaprint (*www.vistaprint.com*), and Paperless Post (*www.paperlesspost.com*) for affordable business stationery.

NO OFFICE? NO PROBLEM!

Following are a few famous companies that grew from humble beginnings—in garages! This demonstrates that it doesn't matter where you start. It matters where you end up.

Amazon

Do any of you happen to remember Amazon before it was the online store that sold everything? Founder, Jeff Bezos, started Amazon in his garage in Bellevue, Washington, imagining it to be nothing more than an online bookstore. Two years later, he took his company public. In May 2014, Amazon was worth $29.7 billion.

Apple

Infamously started by two college dropouts, Steve Jobs and Steve Wozniak, Apple Computers was started by building fifty Apple I personal computers in a garage in Cupertino, California. Later funded by millionaire investor Mike Markkula, Apple Inc. is now valued at more than $500 billion.

Disney

Walt Disney and brother Roy started Disney in Roy's Hollywood home, planning to distribute a series of *Alice Comedies* for $1,500 apiece. Originally named Disney Brothers Cartoon Studio, the name was later changed to Walt Disney Studio and moved into a studio in downtown Hollywood. The Disney empire is now worth $81 billion. Disney is the highest-grossing media conglomerate in the world.

Google

Two Stanford graduates, Larry Page and Sergey Brin, started Google as a research project in the garage of friend, and future Googler, Susan Wojcicki. Wojcicki is now the CEO of YouTube, a Google-owned company. Page and Brin started Google to look into what types of data the Internet held, much different from the Google we know today. It is now the largest Internet company in the world, valued at almost $395 billion.

Mattel

The owners of toy superstars, Barbie and her boyfriend Ken, Mattel began as a picture-frame company out of a garage in Southern California. Founders Harold "Matt" Matson and Elliot Handler (Matt-El) started using picture-frame scraps to create doll-houses, which soon began to sell better than their picture frames. They then turned their production emphasis to toys. Now, Mattel is the highest-grossing toy company in the world.

Yankee Candle Company

Yankee Candle Company began as a Christmas gift for founder Michael Kitteredge's mother. Named *Christmas 1969*, and made from melted crayons, his first candle sparked interest from his neighbors. The first Yankee Candle store opened in 1989 in South Deer-field, Massachusetts. Kitteredge sold the company in 2013 for $1.75 billion.

·✦ Chapter 3's Cinderella Principles ✦·

You might already have a lot of what you need: Discover hidden resources.

Consider crowdfunding: Use platforms like Kickstarter, Indiegogo, and Fundable to raise money from people who believe in your brand.

Find a venture capitalist: Have a unique idea, customers, and a great team.

Find an angel investor: Develop personal relationships first.

Keep it in the family: Clearly outline expectations and boundaries.

Win money in a contest: Find ways to make your project stand out.

Build a business on a budget: Start at home, create a co-op, and take advantage of "free"!

CHAPTER 4

Summon Your Fairy Godmothers

★

NETWORKING

Cinderella's godmother, who saw her all in tears, asked her what was the matter. "I wish I could. I wish I could." She was not able to speak the rest, being interrupted by her tears and sobbing. This godmother of hers, who was a fairy, said to her, "You wish that you could go to the ball; is it not so?" "Yes," cried Cinderella, with a great sigh.

"Well," said her godmother, "be but a good girl, and I will contrive that you shall go."

"Oh, yes," she cried; "but must I go in these nasty rags?"

Her godmother then touched her with her wand, and, at the same instant, her clothes turned into cloth of gold and silver, all beset with jewels. This done, she gave her a pair of glass slippers, the prettiest in the whole world.

Set the Forces of Magic in Motion

Cinderella's fairy godmother, who apparently had spent a lot of time at royal balls and who moved in some pretty heady circles, had all of the special knowledge that Cinderella needed to not only attend the ball, but dazzle, surprise, and delight all who were around her. That impression stayed with everyone who was at the ball.

Without her fairy godmother's specific and detailed instructions, not to mention her impressive skills with a magic wand, Cinderella would never have gotten past the velvet ropes, let alone become queen of the kingdom. Like Cinderella, you need guidance from those who have been there and done that, and can share with you the magical secrets they have learned to open the doors of opportunity. If Zoe Damacela had never signed up for an entrepreneurial class in high school, she would never have realized that she had all the makings of an apparel business right at her fingertips. If Jessica Cervantes's grandma had never taught her to bake, Jessica would never have had the special knowledge she needed to start PopsyCakes. *Your* fairy godmother is close at hand, too.

Take a page from these Cinderella stories, and use the tools in this chapter to go out and summon the forces—magical or otherwise—that you will need to make your dream come true.

Words of Wisdom from Fairy Godparents

"Build relationships and find a way to separate yourself from the crowd. You will be pleasantly surprised with how many doors open for you."

—William Imbo, associate editor at *BoxLife* magazine

Now that you have an idea and a business plan to back it up, it's time to announce your wish to the world and set the forces of magic in motion. This is known as promotion, and it's not an automatic process. You have to put the power of social media, communication, and information into action, and make sure that the people who can help turn your pumpkin into a carriage are relaying your message in the right way.

See and Be Seen by Others in Your Field

Even in today's digital world, getting out and meeting people in your target field face to face is very important. There is nothing like personal contact to establish a lasting relationship with like-minded people who know that they have a lot in common with you. Here are some suggestions for ways to get out and network with the magical forces in your area, and how to make the most out of the situations you find, so that the world is seeing the real and royal you shine through.

* Look for opportunities to join teams, clubs, or groups related to your business. Attend functions and be visible to members, both on- and offline.
* Contribute articles to blogs related to your industry.
* Do more than your share in groups you are part of, or in your current job. Take on tasks others are not keen to do. Be prepared to take risks.
* Look and feel the part of a business owner. Check out your personal appearance. Remember the saying: dress successful, be successful. Be true to your style, but also be professional.
* Read up on how to appraise and improve your skills. Your skills encompass everything you consider something that you are "good" at. For example, you may be skilled at writing code or you might be very organized. Make a list of these skills and be sure you keep them updated. Your skills are worth something, and in order to negotiate a fair salary and figure out where the best use of your skills would be, you have to fairly evaluate yourself. (See Chapter 9 for more information on negotiating.) What are your strengths? What are your weaknesses? Answering these questions will give you an assessment of where you stand within your field of interest. It will also help you prepare for tough questions during an interview or meeting.

★ Be clear on how organizations function. Knowing how a business or organization runs will allow you to have a better idea of how your company should be operating or how you should be behaving within a larger group.

★ Understand your place in the hierarchy of the business world and focus on making the most of your current position. Advancement will only come if you master where you are now. Avoid the arrogance of amateurs. One of the biggest mistakes beginners make is thinking that they are more important than they are. You want to have confidence in yourself, but don't let that stop you from learning.

★ If you know you are interested in something, go after it right away. Don't think too much about it, just do it, or someone else may beat you to the prize.

★ Volunteer your knowledge: Volunteer your expertise in the classroom or on campus to build trust. Don't forget to reach out to the local homeschool community.

Networking Secrets for Royalty in Training

When you are at the beginning of a great business venture, network as much as you can. Include opportunities that aren't specifically in your area of business concern. Success requires that you get involved with all kinds of people, and be known by others. And you never know when you might make that magical acquaintance who turns out to have the key to the kingdom. Networking sets you up for that magical chance encounter with somebody who knows somebody who might be able to offer you a hand, or a helpful piece of advice about your business.

Here are some networking secrets to keep in mind to help you develop and leverage your royal contacts.

Perfect Your Pitch

You should be able to pitch your company in thirty seconds. Investors are short on time and they hear multiple ideas a day. You may be sitting at dinner next to Mark Zuckerberg and this is your one shot. This is where your brand signature and key messages become so important. You don't want to hear the words "time's up" before your pitch is over. Write out your pitch, cut all unnecessary words, then practice it in front of the mirror or for friends. Soon it'll be something you can perform in your sleep—so when the moment arrives for you to talk to a powerful mentor or possible investor, you'll be ready to deliver.

Drive Word-of-Mouth Recommendations

The more people who know and love what you do, the more recommendations you will get, whether it be from online reviews or from people telling their friends and neighbors how fantastic you are. Successful businesses are built on referrals and sustain themselves on positive reviews. So when networking, be sure to share your idea or product with others, encourage them to explore what you have to offer, and then share with *their* friends. Turn everyone you meet into a brand evangelist with your charm and brilliance—and your free samples!

Look for Mentors

Always be on the lookout for potential mentors. Be hungry to learn however and from whomever you can. Don't be intimidated from asking for guidance from people who have more experience or authority than you do. Successful businesspeople are usually generous with advice, particularly with people open to listening.

⋆ Words of Wisdom from Fairy Godparents ⋆

"I find it best to dive right in and learn the hard way."

—Pete Cashmore, Mashable

This is often where your parents or older siblings become a great asset. Ask them if they know anyone you could speak to. If you're going into the same field as your parents, have a serious conversation with them about your future. There are also numerous resources within colleges and universities (such as alumni networks) that can connect you with people in your field. Grab any opportunity you get to speak with an established professional in your chosen field. Use this conversation as a chance to ask questions about where he (or she) started, how he decided on this type of work, what skills are most important to have, and what his favorite part of the job is. Also, remember to follow up and thank him in a timely manner after your conversation.

⁎⁎ Words of Wisdom from Fairy Godparents ⁎⁎

"You may not always have a comfortable life and you will not always be able to solve all of the world's problems at once but don't ever underestimate the importance you can have because history has shown us that courage can be contagious and hope can take on a life of its own."

—Michelle Obama, first African American First Lady of the United States, 2008–

Explore New Market Opportunities

Whenever you are networking with others in and out of your field, remember that this is an opportunity to broaden your thinking, to discover new target markets and new clients, and to think about your business in ways that hadn't occurred to you before. Also, you might discover synergies and cooperative relationships that could enhance your own business offering. For example, your jewelry company might benefit greatly from a partnership with the e-commerce site that your new connection just started. This is a great chance to expand your reach to a larger audience while raising your business's visibility through a partnership. As you're expanding your network, look out for people who may provide new opportunities for your growing company.

Get New Ideas

Meeting other businesspeople and talking about business is a fantastic way to learn new ways to do business. So be curious, be inquisitive, and always be sure to listen carefully for new ideas. What is your next product going to be and who will be using it? How will you continue the momentum of your success? How are other companies doing those things? You might be able to get inspiration or ideas from their plans.

Offer Help to Others

Share solutions, ideas, and encouragement with people you meet who may be facing the same difficulties that you are encountering. Sharing concerns is not admitting defeat; rather, it establishes a rapport that you can rely on for insight and inspiration again and again. Just as you look for mentors, you should offer your help to others behind you in the process. Remember, Cinderella always treated the animals in her forest nicely—and they ended up helping her network! Being kind to others is a good principle to keep in mind as you interact with your customers.

Improve Your Communication Skills

Treat your networking experiences as an exercise in getting out there and introducing yourself to strangers. Learning how to meet and establish a rapport with strangers teaches you how to get your message across effectively and work with different people. Getting a good amount of practice introducing yourself to potential new friends and colleagues will help get you over any shyness or social fears you have, and allow networking to become second nature.

Make Friends as Well as Business Contacts

Although you'll focus on your business, networking can also bring you wonderful new friends who extend into your personal life. Strong friendships are very powerful forces in building your network, so remember that good alliances are always helpful even if they are not specifically involved with your business. You never know when a friend from another field entirely will have a great idea for your business.

Cinderella CEO Q&A

Skyler Bouchard
Food by Skyler blog
www.foodbyskyler.com

Can you tell us a little about your background?

My name is Skyler Bouchard and I dream of eating gourmet dinners and drinking from endless wine lists. While this may seem like a blatant mission towards morbid obesity, it is one of my goals in life to eat at every restaurant in New York City. I started my personal blog so that I can indulge with a purpose and fill everyone in on my dining adventures around the city and the world. I have worked as a writer at the *Daily Meal* and I am the editor-in-chief and founder of *NYU Spoon*, a new branch of the online college food magazine, *Spoon University*. I hope to further my career in the food/entertainment industry and eat like a ravenous lady on TV for all to watch.

Do you have any words of wisdom to share with other young entrepreneurs?

Find something you love and do everything you can to incorporate it into your work. Even if you have a job that isn't your "dream job," pursue your hobby outside of work or try and incorporate it into your daily life. Start a blog or start a new project—anything to keep your great ideas flowing! They will build off of each other and eventually, great opportunities will come.

Do you have any guilty pleasures?

Sometimes after a hard week of work, I love to go on a solo dining adventure. I pick a restaurant that I've always wanted to try and go enjoy a meal by myself to regroup and relax. It's a great way to try something new and have time to myself.

What's the best tip you've ever received on success?

The best tips I've received on success are to fully commit, always keep my word, and envision the outcome. Whether it's schoolwork, internships, extracurricular activities, or my personal website, I fully commit to every project that is on my plate. If I set expectations for myself or make promises to others, I make sure that I stick with it and follow through. In addition to working hard, I always imagine the desired outcome because it helps me stay positive and work towards my goal. Envisioning positive results helps them come true.

Chapter 4's Cinderella Principles

Set the forces of magic into motion: Talk to everyone you can and make meaningful connections.

See and be seen by others in your field: Look for ways to actively participate and connect in your field of interest.

Perfect your pitch: Have a thirty-second elevator pitch ready at all times!

Drive word-of-mouth recommendations: Build a network of referrals, and turn everyone into a brand evangelist.

Look for mentors: Ask for guidance.

Explore new market options: Broaden your audience.

Get new ideas: Be on the lookout for new outlets, products, or services for your company.

Offer to help others: Pay it forward.

Improve your communication skills: Learn how to get your message across effectively.

Make friends as well as business contacts: Make personal connections.

Hear Ye, Hear Ye

★

HARNESS SOCIAL MEDIA

*S*he kneeled down in the ashes next to the hearth and was about to begin her work when two white pigeons flew in through the window. They lit on the hearth next to the lentils. Nodding their heads, they said, "Cinderella, do you want us to help you sort the lentils?"

"Yes," she answered:

The bad ones go into your crop,

The good ones go into the pot.

And peck, peck, peck, peck, they started at once, eating up the bad ones and leaving the good ones lying. In only a quarter of an hour there was not a single bad lentil among the good ones, and she brushed them all into the pot.

Then the pigeons said to her, "Cinderella, if you would like to see your sisters dancing with the prince, just climb up to the pigeon roost." She followed them and climbed to the top rung of the ladder to the pigeon roost. There she could see into the hall, and she saw her sisters dancing with the prince. Everything glistened by the glow of a thousand lights.

Spreading the Word

Cinderella spoke to the birds and mice as she toiled away on her chores, and they kept her motivated and happy. Just as Cinderella got the word out to the animals, you need to share your story with your customers. In this day and age, there are myriad ways to do that. This chapter will explore the most popular and effective methods for reaching your company's audience.

Safety and Privacy Basics for Online Interaction

With the exception of her animal helpers, Cinderella rarely spoke to anyone. She liked her privacy and preferred to spend time alone. She knew this was the best way to protect herself. Once she left a piece of herself out in the open, remember how easy it became to track her down? You could say that Cinderella was a pioneer in protecting her privacy!

Before we talk about specific social media strategies for your company, let's consider safety and privacy. Unfortunately, there are losers out there who might want to steal your ideas or intellectual property—or even jeopardize your personal safety. It's just a fact of life on the Internet—especially for teens. For that reason, you need to be an expert on the privacy features of the social media channels you use. Be sure you know who can see what you post, and be sure you're not posting any personal information that could be misused.

Just as potential employers look at candidates' social media pages when hiring, investors and customers will look at your posts as well. You probably view social media as a place to express yourself and let others know who you are as an individual; these online spaces have become as much a part of your persona as anything else. All of that is great—but it's important to have a good handle on what you're showing others as you build your business.

With social media comes great responsibility. You're probably very tech-savvy, but even with the knowledge that the Internet content is forever, 25 percent of Facebook users don't amend their privacy settings, so those party pictures from last weekend are fully available to potential investors or customers. Many young adults share every detail of their lives on their social profiles, so the line on what is appropriate to post and what should be kept private can be tough to manage. So where do you draw the line?

Ask yourself before you post:

★ Would I want potential investors in my business to see this?
★ Would I want my parents to see this?
★ Does this represent what I want my company to be?
★ Does this represent who I am as an individual?

If your answer to any of these questions is no, keep it to yourself! Some moments are okay to keep private; it does not make them any less real if it is not posted to Instagram or Facebook. Now that you're on your way to being a business owner, you need to think twice about posting what you ate for lunch. Remember, you're basically in public—make sure that persona is always representative of your brand signature and mission.

⋆ ⋆ Words of Wisdom from Fairy Godparents ⋆ ⋆

"I always did something I was a little not ready to do. I think that's how you grow. When there's that moment of 'Wow, I'm not really sure I can do this,' and you push through those moments, that's when you have a breakthrough."

—Marissa Mayer, CEO of Yahoo

A Basic Tool: Your Press Kit

Making a press kit is a great foundation for a social media strategy. Creating one will help you pinpoint key messaging, collect relevant data and contact information, and make sure your company's materials—both on- and offline—have a consistent look and feel. You'll find yourself copying and pasting sections from your press kit to help you build your company's Facebook page, Twitter bio, and so on.

As recently as a decade ago, a press kit meant literally a package of information in a folder sent out to reporters to try to generate interest in a company. The kits were an easy way to share a comprehensive look at a business, but were notoriously cumbersome. A reporter attending an industry trade show could walk away with suitcases full of packets of information from a dozen different companies in a mess of envelopes and loose papers. Lots of it, to be honest, ended up in the recycling bin anyway. Printed press kits have morphed into electronic press kits that live on a website, a blog, or Dropbox, making it easier to handle for both reporters and public relations teams.

Key Elements of a Press Kit

You want your press kit to be one-stop shopping for any writer looking to cover your business. A press kit is constantly evolving—update it as necessary as your company grows and changes. Key elements should include:

★ **Company overview:** What does your company do?
★ **Biographies:** Use this section to talk about your company's founders, CEO, and key players—and have fun with the copywriting. Bios can be playful.
★ **FAQs:** Include a Frequently Asked Questions section to help differentiate your company from your competitors and to give your visitors more details about your policies and practices.

Press Release Tips and Tricks

1. **Include the basics.** Be sure you list the name, e-mail, and phone number of a person to contact for more information, along with that person's title or position with the business. You should also include the date, city where the news is occurring, and a short, punchy headline that captures the essence of your news. If the headline is long, there is the option to create a subheader as well. It is also imperative that you include your company logo.
2. **Get to the point.** This release should not be about the history of your company, but rather the news. There should be a short "boilerplate" at the end of the release that communicates what your history is and what your

company is all about in two or three short sentences. The entire release should be no more than a page.

3. **Include links to your website, blog, and social media pages.** The first thing most journalists and editors will do if they find your story interesting is check out your website or other online presence for more information. This is also important if you're releasing a new product or service—you want to drive traffic to your site so they are able to purchase the items!

4. **Answer this question: "What is the news here?"** Build your story around a news "hook" of some kind, an upcoming event, award, a milestone, or a new product or service. This "news nugget" can also be released early to the press under "embargo," meaning they cannot publish any stories about it until after a certain date. This gives a big media outlet the opportunity for an "exclusive" story. Have your release written a few weeks in advance if you are planning on doing this.

5. **Quote experts whenever possible.** Use direct quotes from key people involved in the news of your press release. This can be an outside source, such as a news outlet or expert, or someone within the company like the CEO or other senior level leader. This lends a first-person feel to your company and news.

6. **Double-check your information.** Make sure that every fact in your release is accurate and can be verified. List sources for statistics you offer. Often the press will pull directly from this release for their stories, so it is important the information is accurate!

7. **Include an About Us paragraph at the end.** This material, also known as a boilerplate, is standard in a press release. It's a short paragraph that captures your company's mission, goals, and brand signature. It will be included in much of your press materials and is often the language used when communicating your company mission to an outsider.

Alerting the Media to Your Press Kit

Once you've assembled your press kit, you can officially release it to the world. Our favorite way to do that is by using the website *www.prnewswire.com*. These guys help you through the process, step-by-step. Once they put your release on the "wire," Google will index so it shows up in Google searches.

Create a Digital Hub for Your Business: Your Website

Online presence is more important than ever in this day and age, so an eye-catching website is necessary to the success of a brand. It is not only the place to debut your brand's identity, but also a way to build brand trust and recognition. A website also functions as a digital hub, where all of your social media links, press, products, and/or services can live in an easy-to-navigate place. This hub becomes *the* place, before and after your product launch, that keeps the company relevant and alive in the minds of consumers.

Websites 101

Here are a few things to bear in mind when you are envisioning your new site:

* Your website address should be posted to your social media channels.
* Your website should be as accessible on a mobile device as it is on a desktop computer.
* Make your website easy to update. Brands are no longer solely purveyors of product; they are also content creators that are constantly updating and conveying their brand story. You need to be able to make updates to your website whenever necessary.
* Make a press kit available for media to download, containing company information, contact information, and any other relevant press material. (Look for more information on press kits earlier in this chapter.)
* Make sure your site's design and structure fit with your overall vision for your product and company.
* Your site should look professional. Often, a visit to a company website is a potential customer's introduction to a business. Think about what you want your first impression to be and build on that idea visually and editorially.

An Example of a Site That Is On Brand

Your website should directly reflect your brand identity. A company that does a really good job of this is Everlane (*www.everlane.com*). Everlane carries their transparent identity in everything that they do; from social content they produce to events they hold, everything accurately and effectively communicates their brand message. Looking at their website can teach you a lot about building a good site of your own.

˙˙ *Words of Wisdom from Fairy Godparents* ˙*˙*

"If you do the things that are easier first, then you can actually make a lot of progress."

—Mark Zuckerberg, Facebook

The Everlane brand has effortlessly carried their brand personality (as the go-to for wardrobe basics with an emphasis on production transparency) into the online space. Their website features clean lines, a basic black-and-white color scheme, easily navigated sections, and a shopping-friendly setup. Their aesthetic carries over to their social media, blog, and e-mail newsletters seamlessly and consistently. This clearly branded and distinct online identity further reinforces what the company is all about and makes it undeniable that clean and basic is how their brand defines itself.

How to Create an Electronic Entourage

Whether you participate in social media or not, it's becoming harder these days not to appreciate its power in publicizing products. A strong social media strategy with a loyal following can create a lot of opportunities for a company to grow its business. Today's socialized "Generation Like" provides a wealth of opportunities for small brands to get the word out about themselves without having to spend big-brand dollars on traditional advertising and promotion. With social media, small is the new big, and the only limit is the scope of your imagination in terms of ways to get the message about you and your brand right to the thought leaders in your field who can make a difference for you.

Understand What You're Building and Why

To successfully build a social following, you need to know what exactly you're trying to build and why your business needs a social media community in the first place. So talk to your fairy godmothers, your friends, and your family and figure out what kinds of things your audience or market might like to hear you post about. Social media is just another way to tell your brand story through images and short bytes; how will your story break out in each social media format?

These are the kinds of questions you should be asking yourself as you go about designing your content for each social media channel. And once you start posting, stay focused and be consistent. Stay on track, and whatever you do keep the focus narrow and tight. Never try to do everything. Be super-specific to your goals!

Here are some general tips to bear in mind no matter what form of social media you are contemplating.

Social Media Rules of Thumb

★ Make your content visual and engaging: think photos, short videos, and an authentic voice to your brand.

★ Promote positive self-expression. Be your best self on social media.

★ Appeal to mobile users. Create an experience that will translate across multiple types of screens.

★ Refresh often and regularly with new and engaging content.

★ Combine personal commentary with brand announcements. Nobody likes social media that looks like a commercial. None of the content you produce should sound like an advertisement (unless it's an actual commercial used once in a while); it should look like a normal blog post. For example, when Brit Morin was opening her MakeShop in San Francisco, she announced it in a mini three-part series detailing all of the features of her new store. It was engaging and fit seamlessly with the rest of her content.

★ Establish a dialogue instead of a monologue. Respond to feedback and comments and try to get a conversation going.

- ★ Repost interesting content from other reliable and relevant sources. Become a resource for insightful, fun, and enlightening content on your area of expertise.
- ★ Be curious, and digitally network with other people in your field who are producing content that is relevant to your brand. Engage with their social media and they and their following will engage with yours!
- ★ Stay on top of the news in your field, and post scoops whenever you can.

Getting Started: The Big Three

You're probably thinking that tens or hundreds of thousands of "likes" and followers are the best measure of a strong following. While these numbers are part of the whole picture, they are not valuable enough on their own. These numbers represent people who have seen your content, but tell you nothing about how they are receiving it, and what they think about what you are saying.

⋆⋆ Words of Wisdom from Fairy Godparents ⋆⋆

"If you've got an idea, start today. There's no better time than now to get going. That doesn't mean quit your job and jump into your idea 100 percent from day one, but there's always small progress that can be made to start the movement."

—Kevin Systrom, Instagram

Our measurement of a strong social following is based on the level of engagement. Establishing an engaged community that talks back, signs up, and subscribes to your content provides a wealth of opportunity not only to learn about your target market but to learn about your content and your brand. Beyond the education you will get about your business and your customer base, an engaged community will help your business extend its audience and reach, both of which can be leveraged through your marketing efforts.

Social networks are more than a place to look for validation of your company's direction; they're a place to make connections and build your own in-real-life personal and professional networks. With so many social networking options, where do you start?

Simple: begin with the three largest social and professional networks—LinkedIn, Facebook, and Twitter.

LinkedIn

Create both a personal and company LinkedIn profile and begin following companies you find interesting. Add your friends, your boss from last summer, even your parents. LinkedIn helps you expand your professional network, both personally and for your company. On your personal page, make sure to include a copy of your resume and keep your profile up to date with your school and work experience.

Your company's profile should house relevant information. Share updates with your followers and make sure you have a current press kit available for those interested to read.

Call to Action

LinkedIn has a lot of features that help you reach out to others who might be interested in your product, services, or campaign. Pay attention to the people you might know feature that offers suggestions for making connections. You can also join larger LinkedIn Groups, which are topic-based. These groups put you in touch with thousands of people who could be potential partners, investors, or customers.

Facebook

Facebook, which began as a closed network for college students, has now become a way for brands to reach out and make friends with their customers and constituencies all over the world. Facebook can be a great tool for small personal brands to launch a digital presence and build a community. Keep in mind that you have to be careful that what you post is something that you are willing to have *everybody* see, including potential customers, vendors, and investors.

Here are some tips to keep in mind when setting up a Facebook page for your brand.

Determine the Creative Foundation

Before you launch the page, you will want to establish a look and feel that matches with your company. Many brands choose to utilize their brand logo for the thumbnail, but the cover photo allows for a little more creativity. Think about colors and design, and remember that you can change your look to match a season or an event, so choose a theme that is versatile, and works with all of your signature moments.

Guidelines

Determine content to establish a tone/voice for your Facebook feed; everything that is written and shared there should be written in this voice and it should be consistent. Think about who your audience is and what voice goes well with it. This will help to determine how copy will be developed and how your brand will engage with its fans.

Have some house rules on dos and don'ts before posting.

Do:

★ Be consistent in your voice.
★ Post regularly. If your readers expect new posts to be up every Tuesday, then every week a new post must be up.
★ Create engaging content with a call to action.

Don't:

★ Post too often.
★ Post off-brand or off-tone content.
★ Post poorly-created content.

Advertise

Within the first month of launching your page, determine how your target consumer will find out about your newly launched Facebook page. Set up a marketplace ad. This is easy to do once you log into Facebook. It can be as low as $.10 per click and stopped at any time.

Evaluate

As you get started with your page, you'll begin to see what posts are performing well with your fans and which ones aren't. You can tell by the level of engagement on each post. For example, if one of your posts gets shared twenty times while your other posts have been getting less love, you'll know which type of post you should be writing. You can also go online and do your homework before posting. There are many resources for learning about social media trends and what types of posts do well overall, like the HootSuite blog (*http://blog.hootsuite.com*) or Social Media Today (*www.socialmediatoday.com*).

Call to Action

A call to action on Facebook usually consists of a poll or a contest. These calls to action can be simple—such as "Share this photo for a chance to win an exclusive necklace from our Spring line!"—or they can be more complicated—such as "Create a Pinterest board inspired by our Back-to-School line and post the link below for a chance to win the whole collection!"

Quizzes are another idea, where users answer a number of questions and in exchange receive some form of premium, such as a discount, or a fun or informative personalized response. If you are a florist or a landscape architect, for example, you might do a "What Kind of Flower Are You?" quiz. Then the results can be posted to the visitor's Facebook feed, along with a picture and a description of their floral personality, whether it be the friendly daisy or the profuse peony.

Immersive exercises like this not only get people engaged with your platform but give them a reason to invite and share your platform with their friends. Getting your readers or customers engaged is important in creating brand loyalists and expanding your reach.

FACEBOOK IN ACTION

C&A: Fashion

C&A (*www.c-and-a.com*), a European clothing store, posted clothes from its new collection on Facebook, encouraging people to "Like" the items they prefer. These numbers were then displayed in real time on the physical hangers of the actual clothing in the store, thus revealing the popularity of each item. This campaign encouraged consumer interaction and opinion, and combined on- and offline social engagement.

Lay's

Lay's (*www.fritolay.com/lays/*) ran crowdsourced campaigns to develop new flavors of potato chips in a number of countries, urging Facebook users to propose and vote on the next flavor. Fans would then receive freebies in return for their input. Rather than simply broadcasting their product, Lay's engaged their fans and encouraged interactions through global contests to find the next best chip in every country, and then broadcast the awards show over their YouTube channel.

Twitter

Twitter began as a quick way to broadcast thoughts in real time. It has now grown to one of the largest and most effective marketing tools in the industry. About 80 percent of businesses big and small are on Twitter, and in 2013, 55 percent of companies used Twitter to vet potential employees. If you are already using Twitter and your profile is littered with inappropriate tweets, make that account private and create a professional Twitter account that will be appropriate for potential investors and customers to view.

The best way to start a Twitter presence for your brand is to post fifty tweets over the course of two to three weeks, before you have any followers. Play with the voice, then review, edit, and delete, until you find the perfect signature tone and content that speaks to your brand and sensibility. Only when you feel good about your existing tweets are you ready to think about followers.

To start building a following, follow every Twitter handle you can think of that may be interested in your brand, or whose brand is of interest to you. This is the best way to start cultivating your following and making affiliations with like-minded people who are passionate about the same kinds of things that you are. They are also a great source for retweets as they will have content that will be of interest to your following as well. Be sure to give credit for the retweet whenever you share! Use Google to find the handles you should be following: "Twitter handles in *x* category." You will have lots of content to learn from, both good and bad. It takes time to get the right mix of fresh content, retweets, and advertisements, but you'll find that balance over time.

Words of Wisdom from Fairy Godparents

"I suffer from the delusion that every product of my imagination is not only possible, but always on the cusp of becoming real."

—Sean Parker, Napster

Advertise

Advertisements on Twitter are more expensive and probably unrealistic for a company just starting out. Another way to garner some Twitter promotion is finding out who the influencers are in your industry or area of interest. These influencers are often willing to do social endorsements for no more than free product, and they can get a large response from their followers. That route is also extremely effective on Instagram. These are inexpensive and effective ways to get the word out to an audience that will be interested in your brand and you are able to have full control over the campaign.

Call to Action

The most popular and effective calls to action on Twitter are asking customers to download your app, asking for a retweet, or asking for a follow. These often require some effort on the part of the consumer, which makes them slightly less effective than a call to action on Facebook.

TWITTER IN ACTION

Ni Nyampinga Magazine

According to the magazine's website, "Rwanda's first magazine for teenage girls, *Ni Nyampinga* [(*www.girleffect.org/explore/the-ni-nyampinga-generation/*)], celebrated its first anniversary by crowdsourcing content from girls from across the country to create the latest issue." This magazine is completely run by women looking to raise a new generation of empowered females in Rwanda. "Issue 6 of the magazine—titled 'Ndashyigikiwe' (meaning 'I have support')—was launched during Umuganda, a national community service day in Rwanda that takes place on the last Saturday of each month." They used tweets to keep momentum going as well as hashtagging. Take a look at *@girleffect* to see what they were able to achieve. They published interviews with girls around the country who were inspiring others, calling themselves the "Ni Nyampinga Generation."

Ben & Jerry's Fair Tweets

Ben & Jerry's (*www.benjerry.com*) launched a campaign to raise awareness of World Fair Trade Day. The promotion filled up unused Twitter characters with messages that promote the cause. Users simply typed out their tweet as you normally would, and Ben & Jerry's populated it with their own messages informing followers about Fair Trade. Their additions to tweets linked to an article promoting World Fair Trade Day. For example, you could tweet "Beautiful spring day!" and Ben & Jerry's would fill the rest of your characters with a message of their own, "I'm sharing my unused Twitter characters to raise awareness for #FairTrade. #FairTweets." This campaign required very little from the user, but helped people feel like they were part of a social justice campaign, and provided Ben & Jerry's with some easy marketing.

CINDERELLA CEO PROFILE

Chelsea Krost
#MillennialTalk
www.twitter.com/ChelseaKrost

Chelsea Krost is a social media success story. At twenty-three, she is an author, radio and television talk show host, and entrepreneur. Chelsea capitalized on skills she already possessed; she used her personality and ability to speak to her peers in an accessible and relatable way as the key to her success. Chelsea was lucky enough to be present during the social media boom, and that became her way to make her voice heard. Through Twitter she gained a following that made the media consider her the "voice of a generation"; at the age of ninteen she was given a book deal. Her tweets focus on women in the Millennial generation, ranging from branded Twitter Chats to articles she finds interesting and inspiring.

Chelsea currently hosts her own talk show for Millennial women (and men) talking about everyday issues. Studio City President Joe Tamanini says "The Millennial audience is often talked about, talked at, but never talked to," and Chelsea was looking to change that.

Chelsea is passionate about giving back and making a change in the world around her. She wants to be a positive role model for the Millennial generation by providing them with a place to talk and learn about being successful in positive ways in a world of negativity. Starting in high school, she was actively involved in philanthropy work and now works with charities like The Trevor Project, Stop Cyber Bullying, and Give A Girl A Chance. Her influence can be seen through her Twitter account (*www.twitter.com/ChelseaKrost*); with over 50,000 followers and hundreds of participants in her weekly Twitter chats she is able to get her message heard around the world.

Chelsea's Twitter followers use the hashtag #MillennialTalk during these chats. She targets young adults who are trying to achieve what she already has—success—by hosting chats with subjects such as entrepreneurship and creating your own opportunities. She has also developed partnerships with relevant brands like ResumeBear, BCBG, Kotex, and MasterCard.

Since the launch of her own show, Chelsea has been asked to speak on *The Today Show* and *Good Day New York*. She has been featured in *Seventeen* and on Yahoo! Her talk show is scheduled to continue filming and expand its broadcast. She continues to expand her social media reach and to further grow her "Millennial" brand.

Other Social Media Channels

Once you have a good handle on the Big Three outlets, it's time to explore other social media channels. Consider which outlets work best for your business and focus on those. Don't try to do *everything* or you won't do *anything* well. If one profile stops getting updated it reflects poorly on the brand, and you don't want that!

Instagram

Though Instagram was originally created for everyday users to upload, edit, and curate photos, it has become a platform for all types of brands to leverage their campaigns through photography, hashtagging, and cross-promotion. To use it effectively, you need to employ several different tactics with your Instagram account.

Original Content

Visual images that capture the spirit and mission of your brand can be an invaluable social media tool for getting people involved with your product or idea. There are lots of photo-editing apps to help you create images that speak creatively, in an original way that truly expresses what you are about, and help you to stand out. Use Instagram to give your followers a behind-the-scenes look at your office or a sneak peek at an upcoming project. With Instagram, daily updates work well, but you should not have more than two or three new photos per day. Your photos don't always have to be of your office or your product, but can be images of things that align with your brand message.

⋆ Words of Wisdom from Fairy Godparents ⋆

"If Google teaches you anything, it's that small ideas can be big."

—Ben Silbermann, Pinterest

The great thing about Instagram is that each feed is different. Your individual perspective makes your Instagram feed inherently *you*. That being said, watch what your competitors are doing, what is working for them and what isn't. The goal isn't to copy their feed, but rather to see what the best types of posts are for reaching your target audience.

Audience-Generated Content

As a result of the ability to utilize hashtags to track and follow user-generated content, brands can engage audiences even more deeply by using their Instagram page as a creative canvas for their followers and potential customers. Promote your dedicated hashtag everywhere you can, use it on all your social posts, ask your customers to use your hashtag when uploading photos of their product or their experience with your company. Follow along with what your customers are posting. People love to be highlighted by a brand they love! Like or comment on the photo, then repost it if it's a really good one.

Share Across Platforms

Another advantage of Instagram is that with the integration of Facebook and Instagram, and the ability to upload photos to Twitter, your brand can increase visibility for its Instagram feed using its more established social media pages. Don't post too often. If you have just posted an image to Twitter via Instagram, wait an hour before your next tweet.

Call to Action

Your Instagram call to action should be based on your hashtag and promoted across your other social channels. For example, Saks ran a campaign last summer using the hashtag #SaksSummer. They asked their followers to post their summer photos for a chance to win a pair of designer sunglasses. This campaign ran for a week; each day one lucky customer got a new pair of sunglasses.

Another way to garner some Instagram promotion is by finding out who the key players are in your industry. These influencers are often willing to do social endorsements for no more than free product, and they can get a large response from their followers.

INSTAGRAM IN ACTION

Adidas

One company that is very successful on Instagram is Adidas (*www.instagram.com/adidas*), a brand that leverages this platform very well. Adidas uses professional-grade photos as a cross-promotion strategy. Instead of opting for the built-in Instagram filters, Adidas uploads high-quality professional photos. When scrolling through their feed, audiences are more likely to pause and check out photos that are not sepia-tinted. So Instagram provides a quick and easy way to stand out from the crowd for Adidas, simply by doing something differently.

Free People

Free People, which is owned by Urban Outfitters and has over a million followers, posts professional photos of their models and products to their Instagram page (*www.instagram.com/freepeople*). In addition, they assign specific hashtags to each type and wash of their jeans, and notify customers of these hashtags when they purchase jeans online and in stores by including the hashtag on a tag with purchase. Customers can upload pictures of themselves with their new jeans, captioned with the specific hashtag, thus providing a conversation and a sense of community with all the people who bought the same jeans. Free People then tracks and uploads the best photos on their website (under additional views of each type of denim), turning their own customers into models and brand evangelists.

YouTube

YouTube is currently the biggest driver of social media available, and many believe it will become the new television. YouTube gives as much reach and access to you, a small brand, as it does to a big brand, provided you consistently create content that people want to see. Not only is YouTube a great and very active outlet for sharing and creating engaging and immersive content about your brand, but a brand can gain wide recognition and loyalty from subscribers, even when the video content is not about the brand at all. Again, it's important to strike a balance of what you post on your channel.

Original Content

Many brands use YouTube to demonstrate their own products—what they are, how they work, and how they can be used.

Related Content

Consider using YouTube to feature events and personalities that are related to or that have relationships with your brand. If your company attends or sponsors an event, such as a festival, upload video highlights. Or you could produce and feature content that simply reflects the style and spirit of the brand, but is created more as entertainment than advertisement. For example, Red Bull sponsors music festivals and extreme sports and creates a large campaign around each video they release. These videos further drive their brand message home and create lifestyle content around their product.

Partnerships

Your company can also use the YouTube community to announce and spread the word about your products. Identifying key influencers in the YouTube community can be great for launching a new product—it not only targets a specific audience, but it also has the potential to reach thousands of people with each mention. For example, Emily Schumann, who writes the Cupcakes and Cashmere blog (*www.cupcakesandcashmere.com*), has a very successful YouTube channel. Since she started her blog, she has done video partnerships with Coach, Estee Lauder, and

Juicy Couture. These videos were all targeted at a different audience than those specific brands usually reach, and they were all focused on a relaunch. Her videos did incredibly well for the brand, each getting around 100,000 views.

Call to Action

Calls to action on YouTube are often done by the host of the video directing the viewer to do something. They can also be done through an overlay on the video, which is a free tool offered by YouTube. You can include links to your website during the video so the viewer is able to click directly through. Also, make sure to include your website and links to your social channels in the video description.

YOUTUBE IN ACTION

Totally Cool Nails

Catherine Rodgers, a girl who "loves to do nail art," created the YouTube channel Totally Cool Nails (*www.youtube.com/user/TotallyCoolNails*), sharing her tutorials on how to create the coolest new looks in nails. Her tutorials were so successful that she attracted over 250,000 subscribers, logging in almost 17 million views. She now has a successful book out!

Red Bull Stratos

The Red Bull Stratos campaign (*www.redbullstratos.com*), which set up an entire mission control and streamed Felix Baumgartner's breathtaking descent from space on its YouTube channel, is a great example of a brand using related content that expresses the spirit of the brand, without ever making a single sales pitch.

EvanTubeHD

EvanTube, which has two channels with over a half a million subscribers, creates original content on kids' toys from a kid's point of view. Evan serves as a product reviewer who appeals to parents, and is a YouTube sensation and a media icon to kids.

An Example of a Social Media–Based Event

One of our former clients, Method, unveiled its Fall 2013 line of products at a preview for media in New York City. To get the party (AKA press preview of their products) started, they asked our company for a strategy to create a memorable event.

So we asked ourselves, what do people think of when they think about Method cleaning products? We decided that people think of Method products as great products, with bright colors and whimsical designs. So here's how we pulled those concepts through and created the campaign.

★ **Social:** Method has an extremely engaged social page—their customers are loyal to the brand and make that known publicly. We hired Oh Snap Smile to set up a digital photo booth. Images could then be shared through social channels featuring a custom Method-branded backdrop. We gave users the option to share to Facebook, Instagram, or Twitter with a dedicated hashtag for the event. We were later able to collect all of the user-generated content and display it on the Method website.

★ **Efficacy:** Guests were walked through a branded room featuring Method's Fall 2013 line where they were able to test products.

★ **Results:** More than thirty attendees from various top tier media outlets attended, including online editors from *Bon Appétit, Us Weekly, People Style Watch, W, Real Simple, Ladies' Home Journal,* the *New York Times, House Beautiful, Lonny,* and *Shape.* We had a ton of social media presence through a special hashtag #cleanhappy.

★ **What to notice:** Engagement on Method's Facebook page (*www.facebook.com/method*) is strong compared to many other businesses.

★ **What to learn:** Method seems to understand their audience very well. Fans know that Method makes the content because it is all authentic to their brand. They don't ever feel as if Method is spamming them or forcing new product upon them. Since Method's brand is based on transparency, their social content reflects that. Sticking with this simple formula allows their followers to know what to expect, which decreases the chance of them "disliking" Method's page due to distracting content.

★ **What to do:** Figure out what your audience wants and deliver consistent, quality content (photos, videos, articles, data) to them. On top of that, engage your audience by asking questions on your social channels.

✦ Words of Wisdom from Fairy Godparents ✦

"A hard thing is done by figuring out how to start."

—Rand Fishkin, SEOmoz

Blogging

Many young entrepreneurs start out by creating a blog to track their passions and work. Some of these blogs gain a huge following and become successful businesses in their own right. Whether you're interested in starting a blog or in bringing yours up to the next level, here are some tips that should be useful.

Technical Stuff: The Basics

★ **Select a domain and hosting site.** The first step is to register your domain name—you'll find lots of companies online that do that. You can also check out tumblr.com; they will host for free.

★ **Choose a theme.** A good theme—color scheme, font styles, and so on—gives you the look and feel you want for your blog. Many hosting sites allow you to design your blog exactly how you want it to look.

★ **Add "feed" capabilities.** Set up a free Feedburner account so people can subscribe to your site via e-mail and RSS subscriptions. That way, they're alerted when you've posted something new.

★ **Consider plug-ins.** Use Google Analytics for WordPress and really simple Facebook and Twitter share-button plug-ins. Since human beings are intrinsically wired to share value, it's important to make your posts easy to share with others.

Share That Content

First, the golden rule is to write five to ten blog posts first. Share those within a tight network of friends or colleagues and get feedback. Once the blog is in decent shape and you feel ready to share it with the rest of the world, make sure you do the following:

1. **Explain your blog.** On the front page of your blog, give visitors more information about what you can do for them.
2. **Think of your audience first.** As you are thinking of blog topics, make sure the information will be helpful to your target customer.
3. **Build relationships online and develop trust.** If you want friends online, you must be friendly first. If you want people to spread your blog posts on Facebook or Twitter, or subscribe to an RSS feed, you need to spend time sharing other people's content and building relationships online first.
4. **Be original.** Being transparent and vulnerable is a great way to establish a relationship with your readers. Teach them new stuff and be entertaining. Have that signature content so your readers start to get who you are.
5. **Don't add "fluff."** Resist the temptation to fill in content with meaningless posts. Your products and services will sell themselves if you create an effective and helpful blog.
6. **Diversify.** Diversity rules in the Magic Kingdom. In addition to written articles, add podcasts, videos, and social content. Keep those video posts short—no more than one minute! Less is more.
7. **Add a Call to Action.** At the end of every post, ask a question of your readers to get them to add a comment to the post.
8. **Be interesting.** Pose questions that are mysterious, funny, curious, thoughtful, or controversial. We love what Refinery29 (*www.refinery29.com*) is doing these days with their headlines.

One last thing. You may not want to share your blog with your parents, but if you are under twenty-one, they do have some legal rights and obligations. We recommend that you do give them the web address of your blog, and it's a good idea to talk with them about what you're doing and reassure them that you understand basic safety and privacy rules.

✦ Chapter 5's Cinderella Principles ✦

Learn safety and privacy basics for online interaction: Take control of things you post on the Internet.

Create a digital hub for your business: Make your website easily accessible to you and your customers.

Create an electronic entourage: Use the power of social media to deliver messages to your audience.

Understand what you're building and why: Tell your story on social media in an effective and interesting way.

Master social media rules of thumb: Be engaging, positive, and accessible.

Get started on the Big 3—LinkedIn, Facebook, Twitter

Move on to others—Instagram, YouTube

Consider starting a blog: Many young entrepreneurs began their ventures this way!

CHAPTER 6

Make a Grand Entrance

LAUNCH YOUR BRAND

She promised her godmother to leave the ball before midnight; and then drove away, scarcely able to contain herself for joy. The king's son, who was told that a great princess whom nobody knew had arrived, ran out to receive her. He gave her his hand as she alighted from the coach, and led her into the hall, among all the company. There was immediately a profound silence. Everyone stopped dancing, and the violins ceased to play, so entranced was everyone with the singular beauties of this unknown newcomer.

Nothing was then heard but a confused noise of, "How beautiful she is! How beautiful she is!"

Making an Entrance Fit for a Princess

When Cinderella finally rolls up to the palace and enters the ball, she doesn't just walk in the door and head for the coat check like any old princess. Cinderella makes a grand entrance that causes a hush to fall over the whole palace ballroom, which is not exactly an intimate space.

From the moment she steps onto the royal red carpet, Cinderella has everybody staring at her and wondering who this mysterious and exotic creature might be. And when she leaves, people are searching the countryside for her just to catch another glimpse. Cinderella is able to make such a splash because she has successfully implemented all of the elements of a successful launch campaign. The result is instant and immediate brand recognition, so to speak.

⋆ Words of Wisdom from Fairy Godparents ⋆

"I don't believe in guilt, I believe in living on impulse as long as you never intentionally hurt another person, and don't judge people in your life. I think you should live completely free."

—Angelina Jolie, actress and philanthropist

Cinderella teaches us that first impressions, and making the most of those impressions when they happen, are big moments in the life cycle of any business. After all, the public perception of your brand begins at your launch. Planning and executing a memorable grand entrance require thought, skill, creativity, and a little bit of magic. Most important, you need a well-devised plan for an event that serves your ultimate goals and that will get the right people whispering to their friends about the amazing new princess who has just entered the ball.

Cinderella's Pre-Launch Principles

Before Cinderella can make a grand entrance, she has to go through a number of steps to make sure that when she walks through those doors, she will create an unforgettable and favorable impression that will launch her into the next phase of her brand life. She has to find the right dress and the right crystal carriage, and must attend to even the minutest detail, down to the tiny white mice as footmen.

What Cinderella teaches us is that the secret to a successful launch is a successful *pre*-launch. It's important to pick the right venue, the right time, the right activities, and the right mix of people. Once you have settled the royal guest list, you need to reach out and prepare them, as well as yourself, for the time of their lives. Cinderella offers lots of guidance to help you have a successful pre-launch, so that by the time you make your entrance at the ball all you have to do is dance. Here are her principles:

1. Create a Party That Suits Your Purpose
2. Timing Is Everything
3. The Sticky Factor
4. Match Your Party to Your Pocketbook
5. Creating the Royal Guest List
6. It's the Little Things
7. Don't Forget Drinks!
8. Say It with Swag
9. Start Spreading the News
10. Getting the Media on Board
11. Launch Day!
12. Make a List and Check It Twice

No matter what kind of party you plan, expect that it'll be a lot of work to pull off. Exactly what type of work you'll need to do depends on the type of event you're hosting. Something that has been extremely popular lately has been outdoor "garden parties." Boutique wedding company LOHO Bride (*www.lohobride.com*) and Free People (*www.freepeople.com*) have been leading the way for these fun, inexpensive events. For this type of event, you will need to secure an outdoor location, preferably with an emergency rain setup, food and drink vendors, a florist, photographer, and, of course, the guest list. Make a list of every single thing that will need arranging, from booking a workable venue to securing any necessary licenses that may be necessary (for example, a performance license or a license to run a lottery). Thinking carefully through all the moving parts that your vision will demand and making a prioritized list to guide you through the process are crucial components of any successful event. Look at the end of this chapter for a handy checklist that helps you keep track of everything.

Let's look at all the components of a successful launch party in more detail.

Create a Party That Suits Your Purpose

The type of event that suits your brand will be determined by a number of variables such as your budget, the outcome you are trying to achieve, and whether you are looking for swift or long-term success.

Brand Launches That Worked

A launch often involves more than just one event on one night, but encompasses an entire campaign that builds on expressing the brand story. Here are two launches that did a great job of promoting the product while highlighting the brand signature.

Dove Soap

Dove is a skin care company that has always believed in using real women for their ads. They always make it a point to speak to and reflect women of every shape, size, and color in their campaigns and ads because their target market is real women of all shapes and sizes.

Dove's national "Show Us Your Skin" campaign asked women from all over the world to upload their photos for a chance to participate in their campaign. These photos were made available online, as well as on billboards in New York City's Times Square. Within one year, this initiative resulted in double-digit lifts in their brand recognition as well as thousands of consumer submissions. The campaign was covered in every major media outlet within three days of the launch of the campaign.

The Five-Dollar Foot-Long Fashion Show

Subway—yes, the Jarod sandwich brand—wanted to gain the attention of fashionistas and fashion bloggers during New York Fashion Week. In order to launch themselves into a new market that doesn't normally think about stopping by for a five-dollar foot-long, the sandwich chain partnered with Nolcha Fashion Week—an event that celebrates independent fashion designers. Subway hosted a fashion show featuring designs made entirely out of items from Subway restaurants, including sandwich wrappers, plastic sandwich bags, gift cards, straws, salad bowls, pizza boxes, and cookie bags. Subway received more than 20 million "likes" on Facebook for this one event, and we will never forget it!

The Blair Witch Project

To create buzz for the horror flick *The Blair Witch Project*, the filmmakers distributed footage to college campuses and presented them as real video diaries. The Independent Film Channel also played clips, labeling them documentary instead of fiction. This PR stunt created tons of intriguing gossip about the film. It is important to think out of the box!

The Power of Shorts?

Sophie Sieck, one of our Advisory Board members, reported back to us on a campaign based on stamps for an apparel startup she helped launch. At the launch event, everyone was told to wear shorts. The event started at 11:00 A.M. and everyone stamped the back or front of their thighs with a stamp that said "Shorts rule" and included the logo of the company. She was able to hashtag the event and garner a ton of social media around this inexpensive launch held at a local art gallery—an inexpensive yet creative way to hold an event for just a few hundred dollars. Her friend owned the art gallery, so the only payment was for the stamps and food. Look for spaces with minimal (or no!) rental fees—that'll save a huge chunk of money.

Timing Is Everything

As Cinderella's own launch plan clearly illustrates, timing is a key element in any grand entrance—and exit! So once you have decided what kind of event you are going to create for your launch, start thinking carefully about picking the date. A launch is often a make-or-break moment for a small company. Effective timing is critical, so you can attract lots of customers when you're ready, thereby optimizing profit.

When Will Your Business Be Ready?

Ideally, you should leave at least six months to prepare for the big day. Remember, a successful launch means a successful pre-launch, so the more time you have to prepare and promote the event, the more successful it is likely to be. This isn't to say that planning an event to take place in six weeks' time is impossible, because it isn't—but it will require considerable effort to ensure that everything is arranged properly in such a short space of time.

A factor that may affect the timing of your business launch is market trends. Is demand for the type of product you offer on the rise or is your product on the verge of fading into the sunset? If your business will specialize in a certain type of product, the ideal situation would be to enter the market while demand is still on the rise or, at the very least, stable.

✦ Words of Wisdom from Fairy Godparents ✦

"I don't have big ideas. I sometimes have small ideas, which seem to work out."

—Matt Mullenweg, WordPress

You also need to be aware of regional factors, such as the number of nearby businesses that offer similar products and services. If several established companies have recently announced plans to sell similar products and services, then you will need to question your ability to compete locally. With the presence of the Internet, you have the option to become a fully online business if the market would be too challenging locally. However, if you are planning on opening your own brick-and-mortar store, local competition will be something you need to pay attention to. Think of your two local coffee shops. Is there one you strongly prefer? How about your friends and family; which coffee shop do they frequent? You want *your* shop to be the town favorite. Make sure your opening is unique. Often, getting involved in a local charity or community project makes a great tie to your area that will make people remember your business. Showcasing local products also goes a long way within the community.

One of the most important factors in timing the launch of your business is to ask yourself how prepared YOU are to open your doors to the world. If you have rushed through the preparation process without laying a solid foundation, then now is definitely not the right time to launch your company. Take the time you need to research your market, understand your product, and nail down your procedures. Only then is it time to set the date for your launch.

✶ Words of Wisdom from Fairy Godparents ✶

"If you feel like you're lost and have no idea what you're doing, don't worry . . . no one else knows what they're doing either."

—Jordan McMullen, leather development & commercialization manager at Coach

Launch Dates

Here is a list of questions you should ask yourself about the dates you are considering for your royal ball.

1. Are there any other events happening on or around the same date that your guest list is likely to be attending?
2. Is there any kind of holiday or current happening you can tie in to to increase press coverage?
3. Is your date at a time when your guest list is in town and likely to be available?
4. Does your product/brand have an overall theme that relates to a specific date?

5. Does your media partner have any upcoming events that you would be able to be a part of? Your media partner will be an influential, local media outlet. This may be the major newspaper in your city, or the major magazine. A media partner could also be a larger blog or website.

6. Are any major publications running specific stories that could tie in to your launch?

The answers to these questions might help you narrow your options to a few dates that will best suit your company and your ability to spread the word about its launch.

The Sticky Factor

The theme of your launch event should embody your brand and should stick in the mind of every consumer. Your launch should get the public excited about what your brand is all about, and should be "sticky"—have staying power—so your impact lasts long after the band has left the stage.

You can make your event sticky in a variety of ways. Some launches are memorable because of a unique location or innovative theme. Others are made stickier through strategic media partnerships. For example, a San Francisco company would benefit from a partnership with a known San Francisco publication such as 7x7 (*www.7x7.com*). Not only is the partner able to get the word out through their network, but they will also provide media coverage pre- and post-event, which is part of the launch event end goal.

A good example of a sticky high-concept launch is Warby Parker, a company that makes eyeglasses and sunglasses. Warby didn't launch with a typical party; instead, they took their launch across the United States. The Warby Parker Class Trip stopped at cities across the country to spread the word about their online business in a redone, vintage school bus that doubled as an eyeglass store complete with an optometrist. Staying true to the integrity of their quirky, fun brand that supports vision and reading for everyone, they turned an old school bus into a classic university library and allowed attendees to try on glasses or flop down with a classic book or comic. What made this launch so sticky and successful was the ability to communicate their brand message both on- and offline, bridging the digital and physical worlds. The use of a physical space to introduce their online-only product to consumers created a relationship with customers that wouldn't have been achieved through a digital campaign. At each stop they involved a local company, such as Camp Wandawega in Chicago and Greenwich Vintage footwear in Minneapolis, and they highlighted these small businesses on their website and at their events in each city. By getting the local communities involved at each one of their stops, they made consumers feel involved in a brand that previously existed only in cyberspace.

CINDERELLA CEO PROFILE

Bella Weems
Origami Owl
www.origamiowl.com

Bella Weems from Chandler, Arizona, thought up the idea for Origami Owl, a direct sales jewelry company that connects independent designers with buyers, when she was only fourteen years old. Since then her company has grown into a multimillion-dollar enterprise, connecting thousands of designers nationwide.

Bella created Origami Owl to make enough money to buy a car for her sixteenth birthday. She came up with the idea of making her own jewelry and then launched her business, selling her signature Living Lockets everywhere and anywhere—at house parties, local jewelry shows, and small boutiques in her area. Today, her business is valued at $250 million, so we are betting she got her dream car on her sixteenth birthday.

Match Your Party to Your Pocketbook

It's easy to get carried away when you are planning your own brand launch. Bear in mind that there are many hidden costs that you would never think of, so be sure to do your research when it comes to pricing out your ideas. Hidden costs may include cost of parking at the event space, late add-ons to your menu, postage for your invitations, and last-minute miscellaneous expenses (Do you need a police officer at the door? Do you need an assistant to keep track of RSVPs?). Make sure that you ask for transparent estimates that include all charges.

Most important, be realistic about what you are able to spend on a launch. You don't want to spend your entire annual sales prediction on the launch party, or you won't stay in business. It is important to budget at least $500 per fifty guests at an event so you have at least water and juice! Startup events can be lean and intimate, geared to the audience you are trying to attract. We never spend more than $5,000–7,000 on an event for a startup for around seventy-five people. This includes space rental, catering, a DJ, valet parking, and help at the event. So be prudent, and as Cinderella teaches us, get the biggest bang for your buck at every opportunity.

Here are some tips for penny-pinching princesses on how to throw a sufficiently royal event without breaking the bank.

Look for Off-the-Beaten-Path Locations

Picking the proper venue for your event is crucially important and will be determined by the nature and purpose of your event, as well as your budget. Renting the grand ballroom at the Plaza might work for *Fortune* 500 companies, but as a startup company, you'll need a little more creativity to arrive at the right venue at the right price. Do your homework, and think creatively, because a party can happen anywhere a group of people can gather together for a singular purpose (and nibble treats).

Some of the most incredible, memorable, and just downright cool events we've been to were held in completely unexpected places. Local parks with catered foods and waitstaff can be as welcoming as any venue. If you have spent time making your office glam, look no further for your event venue—lots of companies have held events at their offices with great success. Here are some other ideas.

* Look on Google for event locations in your city.
* Engage your network on Facebook and ask for suggestions for cool places to throw an event. Hold a contest to see which of your alternative venue options people like the most.
* Public buildings often have large rooms available for rental.
* Look out for parks and open spaces you may be able to use for free.
* Has a new restaurant opened in your town? Ask if they would be willing to sponsor or host an event at their new location in exchange for free promotion.
* Spend a day exploring your area and finding cool places off the beaten path. Then talk to the people involved with the best places to see if an event like yours is possible.
* Check out L.A.–based startup Eventup.com (*www.eventup.com*), which lists venues around the country for rent and will help you work around issues like location and budget constraints.

Once you've narrowed your ideal list to a few spots, talk to others who have had events in spaces that you are interested in. Ideally, see the options in person. If this isn't possible, do your homework online and talk to others about the space on social networks.

CINDERELLA CEO PROFILE

Catherine Cook
MyYearbook.com and cofounder of MeetMe
www.meetme.com

*"To any entrepreneur: if you want to do it, do it
now. If you don't, you're going to regret it."*

—Catherine Cook

When Catherine Cook was fifteen years old, she started up a company called MyYearbook.com with her brother. What started as a simple digital way for people to meet others who had gone to their high school became a huge sensation when Catherine appeared with Facebook founder Mark Zuckerberg to pitch her business idea to Barry Diller in a competition called "What Would Barry Buy?" Barry selected Catherine's concept as the business concept that he would buy, which catapulted her company to national visibility; just three years later, MyYearbook sold for $100 million. This Cinderella CEO has clearly demonstrated how to make a grand entrance, and the power of the right launch timing and partnership to instantly establish brand recognition.

Creating the Royal Guest List

For a successful launch, you'll want to invite your fans, friends, and contributing artists, as well as industry influencers in technology, social media, and startups. So how do you get these people to show up?

In order to find people interested in your product, do some research on LinkedIn, Facebook, Twitter, and Instagram. These search feeds are an incredible resource for finding just about anyone who does anything. Many people cold-call these days through social media, so don't worry if you don't know somebody, just reach out! You may even be surprised at the response you get. For example, are you hoping to get the food critic from your local newspaper out to your opening? Send him an e-mail, and if you don't hear back, follow up with a tweet. If you're looking for a local designer to come take a look at your work, a handwritten card mailed to his or her home would be nice. It needs to feel personal. If you really want this person there, don't be afraid to make the effort.

You can also set up your event on EventBrite (*www.eventbrite.com*), a social-media-friendly (and free!) event management site. EventBrite will keep track of your RSVPs, help you spread the word through social media, create personalized invitations, and create a guest list you will be able to check at the door. To get the word around, start by reaching out to your existing social networks, mobilizing your Facebook fans and Twitter followers, and corresponding with your current partners. Next, it's time to share the details with industry influencers by sending out e-cards and printed invitations to as many of your VIPs as possible.

Bringing the right people to the party and making sure that they attend in sufficient numbers is a crucial factor in achieving your desired outcome. There's nothing worse than standing in the middle of a grand ballroom that has twelve people in it. Here is a checklist of things that you should consider when making out your royal guest list and some ideas for how to make sure that you will fill the house.

★ Ask yourself: What do I want to accomplish with this event? Your answer will help you determine the appropriate crowd to target. Do you want people to actually buy or order things at this event? Invite a group of people who are ready to shop. Promote the event as a sale. Make sure your guests are aware that this event will have products ready to sell. Do you want it to start a conversation to catch the eye of investors? Invite the media and make sure they know you are looking for coverage. Talk to them and give them a clear picture of what your company is doing so they are able to write about it later. Are your goals more focused around creating a social media following? Invite a young, hip crowd. Create a dedicated hashtag for the night. Make sure your guests are aware of the hashtag prior to the event and display it at the event.

★ When hosting events in major cities, consider the transportation alternatives and timing of travel from a variety of locations. Is it easy for your target guests to get to the event from their offices? What about getting home at the end of the night? Not everyone will have a car and be able, or willing, to travel far.

★ Ask for feedback about plans for your event; take that into consideration and make changes for the big day. If you're planning to throw an event on a Tuesday night and your peers are telling you that doesn't make sense, change it to Thursday. Ask for input on your decorations and overall theme—does anyone have any additions or changes? This is the time you have to perfect your event before the greater public is introduced to your brand, so take all the input you can get! Most things (except for catering, photographer, space, and alcohol) can be coordinated relatively close to the event.

★ Look through your mailing list for relevant, industry-specific groups that can double as your media partners. Having engaged partners associated with your event attracts loyal customers and adds legitimacy to your event. If you are starting a home décor e-commerce store, it would benefit your new brand greatly to have a media partner like *ELLE Décor*. Although that may seem out of reach at this early stage in your business, you never know! A big name to cross-promote your event with will help with attendance and guarantee you some media coverage.

★ Be a facilitator by connecting guests with one another during and after your event.

★ Create a Facebook page or Twitter account for your attendees to build a community around your event and keep them excited about the next one.

★ Use a dedicated hashtag to promote your event that is shared with guests before, during, and after the launch.

★ Create a Facebook contest or giveaway related to the event.

It's the Little Things

The devil and the divine are both in the details. It truly is the little things that make or break a successful launch party, so get creative. Not only will an attention to fine detail maximize the impact you can make, but creativity is currency and can save you lots of money over more traditional approaches to making a splash.

Here are a few ideas for creative detailing:

★ Candy stations with a mix of treats in cool jars, which have been common at a lot of fashion industry parties, look pretty and always impress.

★ Servers with drinks or snacks waiting for guests upon arrival make a big impression for a small price.

★ Balloons are always a festive, inexpensive option. Tape the strings of helium balloons in your company colors to the floor at various heights along a wall, or buy balloons in unique shapes and fill with regular air, then scatter on the floor along the edges of your event space.

★ Live performances always dress up an affair. Find an up-and-coming crooner who will agree to play for free in exchange for generous promotion.

Don't Forget Drinks!

First off, the bar doesn't have to be stocked with alcohol. Create a custom "mocktail" that reflects your brand identity. Make sure you have water, sparkling water, and at least one flavored drink. Tangerine soda mixed with limeade is a perfect drink!

If your guests will be twenty-one or older, you probably want to have a bar at your party. What makes for a good party bar? Good drinks, lots of selection, and a fast line. Mixology and signature drinks are popular, so why not invent your own drinks menu that reflects the spirit of your brand?

Also, nothing ruins an event like a couple of ugly drunks. So, one of the ingredients that every good party bar should have is responsible service, and snacks. You don't want your guests to drink on an empty stomach, so go by Costco and pick up a few party platters and convince a nearby restaurant to donate some dessert.

Say It with Swag

Everybody loves a little takeaway or something special at the end of an evening. Party favors or goody bags can be inexpensive and easy to make. It doesn't take an abundance of free items or anything elaborate; you can get by with something small that says "Thanks for joining us" and "Don't forget to look for our product!" on it. This is also an opportunity to develop partnerships with local retailers, restaurants, and companies who may be willing to donate their products for your goodie bag in exchange for promotion and publicity. See the following for some examples of great swag bags:

* **If you're a tech startup:** The people attending your event have likely been sitting in front of a computer for a long period of time. Give your guests a mini-relaxation or mini-unplug kit.
* **Ask yourself: What will people keep using?** Create some custom swag that your guests will use over and over again, and thus be reminded of your brand over and over! Many companies create inexpensive tote bags, key chains, or pens.
* **Consider food:** GroupMe, a mobile-to-mobile chat app, stationed a grilled-cheese truck outside their event at SXSW in 2012; all their guests left with a gooey snack and a good taste in their mouth.
* **Create a digital gift:** Give your guests a download for a branded digital magazine, an e-book, an app, or a song that they will be able to share and access long after the event.

Start Spreading the News

Once you know exactly what you need to do to get a successful event organized, and know that you can actually pull everything off, you can start promoting it. The most cost-effective way to do this is by sending press releases to as many as possible local (or national, if the event demands this) newspapers, broadcasters, publications, and other relevant organizations. Of course, in addition to using press releases, you can use other promotional methods if your budget allows. Advertising, direct mailshots, and even Internet promotion can all be used to good effect for many events if you have the money available.

In addition to one-off coverage, ongoing publicity is essential. Once everything is in place and the event itself is sorted out, aim to get even more publicity by contacting the feature editors of newspapers, magazines, and television shows and inviting them to attend and cover the event. If the event is something that will be of interest to their readers or viewers, you can get coverage before, during, and after the event—thus turning perhaps a one-day PR event into a publicity campaign that will span several weeks.

Here are some tips for how to maximize publicity for your event, and announce to the world that you're coming up!

Writing an Effective Press Release

Some components that successful press releases need to include are:

* **Your logo:** Build recognition by including your logo at the top of your release.
* **The news:** The most important rule for writing a press release is to make sure that it's centered on a single, newsworthy topic.
* **A concise headline:** Search engines rely heavily on page titles to determine ranking, and your press release's headline is its page title. Your headline should be between five and eighteen words. Search engine results often limit titles to around sixty-seven characters.
* **Meaningful links:** Use links in your release to direct your audiences to relevant additional content.
* **Multimedia:** Embedded images or video increase your release's reach in search engines.
* **Follow-up information:** Include your contact details.

⋆⁺⋆ Words of Wisdom from Fairy Godparents ⋆⁺⋆

"Everything started as nothing."

—Ben Weissenstein, Grand Slam Garage Sales

Sample Press Releases

We launched this fun travel startup that was founded by a few guys who met in school.

Introducing Mosey: A Simple Way to Create Curated Day Trips for Your Friends, Fans, and Fans-to-Be

SAN FRANCISCO, CA—(Marketwired—Apr 18, 2013)—Mosey announces the launch of mosey.com, a platform of mobile and social micro-guides that enable users to create and share the perfect day trip (Mosey).

A Mosey is the best 4 hours in any given city. With Mosey, you can easily curate a custom itinerary connecting your favorite places and things to do. Whether it's a hot date night, Sunday pub-crawl with the boys, a bachelorette party to remember, or a weekend trip to a new city, Mosey captures all your best experiences, both in your own backyard and abroad. It is also the perfect answer to the question, "Hey, I'm coming to your town. What should I do?"

Looking for something new to do on a lazy Sunday? Explore the Mosey library to check out a hidden gem in your own city. Planning a trip? View your friends' or trendsetters' Moseys for a great adventure in a new city.

"Almost all other sites are about individual places, such as a restaurant, surrounded by a flurry of reviews and ratings contributed by 100 different people. Places are just the building blocks of Mosey as we deal in experiences. At Mosey, the person is at the center . . . a person surrounds themselves with their favorite adventures (Moseys), the places that make up those Moseys and the people they choose to follow," said Eric Persha, cofounder.

Designed to fit on all your mobile devices, use Mosey on the go to access photos, directions and personalized tips wherever you are. This mobile guide can also be easily shared with your friends and social community. No downloads necessary, just click the link on any of your devices and you are ready to Mosey.

About Mosey

Mosey. Make Epic Plans.

Mosey is the perfect answer to the question "Hey, I'm coming to your town. What should I do?" Use Mosey to create a step-by-step guide to your favorite places and activities. Then share it with anyone, anywhere. Whether you've got cabin fever at home or you're traveling abroad, Mosey on over to your next adventure.

Following is a good example of a press release announcing a specific announcement with a brand ambassador.

adidas NEO Label Signs Selena Gomez As New Style Icon And Designer

Selena Gomez gets mischievous on the streets of Los Angeles to launch her new fashion collaboration

Los Angeles woke up to some colorful hijinks today with bright green paint, posters, and streamers spread across the city as actress, recording artist, and designer, Selena Gomez and a band of teens celebrated her new partnership with adidas NEO Label.

The mischievous and fun antics playfully announced that teen lifestyle brand, adidas NEO Label has appointed Selena Gomez as its new global style icon and guest designer through a three-year partnership until the end of 2015.

Selena will work with NEO to design and develop seasonal ranges that consumers and her fans will love, beginning Fall/Winter 2013. She will also be the face of four seasonal collections throughout the year and will appear in print, digital, retail, and outdoor campaigns to debut in February 2013. She will identify her favorite pieces, the first of many opportunities for Selena to communicate her personal style with fans.

Selena Gomez said adidas NEO Label is a new brand for teens and their looks are fun and easy to wear, making it a perfect brand for her lifestyle.

"It is a great partnership for me because NEO really cares about style and having fun with fashion and allowing you to be yourself. This is something that's always been important to me and is important to my fans, too: knowing they can express themselves through wearing whatever clothes they want and feel good about themselves.

"I am really enjoying being involved with the design process and NEO is letting me have fun with this. I get to wear the clothes first and have a voice and an opinion and I can't wait to see the results of our new collection. I'm excited that it also allows my fans to be involved and they can come with me on this journey," she said.

Hermann Deininger, Chief Marketing Officer adidas Brand, said the fundamental inspiration for adidas NEO Label is teenage culture – seeking excitement, adventure, and unexpected surprises.

Visit www.adidas.com/NEO *to stay up to date on all things NEO.*

Who Should Get Your Release

Your press release should be distributed via e-mail to everyone you have contacted about your business up to that point. It should be electronically available on your website. It should also be sent via e-mail to any media that covers topics related to your brand. (These can be found through a Google search.) Make sure to hit your local paper, and take a look at TechCrunch and FastCompany to cover your startup launch. Ask if local event blogs would be willing to pull content from the press release to create a post for their audience. If you are sharing your party invite externally, make sure you are keeping track of the guest list electronically (via EventBrite) so guests don't have to speak directly to you to attend.

CINDERELLA CEO PROFILE

Madison Robinson
Fish Flops
www.fishflops.com

"I believe in charitable giving, being happy, and helping others. Act on your creativity."

—Maddie Robinson

Houston teenager Madison Robinson developed her sea-creature-adorned flip-flops with battery-operated lights when she was eight years old, living near the beach in Galveston Island, Texas. Her father, a former banker turned T-shirt designer, helped her turn her drawings into a product and get samples made. She launched her new business at a trade show, and got orders from thirty stores on the very first day. But Madison wasn't done yet. Madde is also a pro with social media marketing: From her Twitter account, *@FishFlops*, she got the young daughter of *Entertainment Tonight* host Nancy O'Dell to wear the shoes, and also captured the attention of HSN fitness personality Tony Little.

Getting the Media on Board

Once you've spread the word about your event, it's time to go the extra mile with the press to try to secure good coverage and promotion for your product or service. It is important to use your best magic with the press! To create enchanting press coverage, it is imperative to give the press special treatment at the event. Try to find images of relevant people ahead of time so you can recognize them at the event and give them a bit more attention. To get these big names to attend in the first place, it is imperative that you give them a reason to come to your soiree. Here are some ideas for getting the big names behind you.

* Make sure all the press receive some sort of press release or media alert about the event.
* Invite press to try your service or use your product prior to the event.
* All fairy tales are stories meant to be told, so get some buzz going by offering an exclusive interview or behind-the-scenes footage of your brand being developed.
* And finally, don't forget post-event followup! Send the press all your materials again with images from your event so they have everything they need to write it up.

Gift Product to Influencers Before Launch

Give samples of your product to influencers, like bloggers, before you launch so that early articles written about you contain third-party product validation. This will give more confidence to other outlets that want to write about your product and enable them to endorse you with more enthusiasm. For example, if Refinery29 were to cover your product, your company would become a reputable brand within the beauty and fashion blogger worlds. The same goes for technology coverage in TechCrunch or Gizmodo—it gives other influencers the validation they need to see you as a real company with viable product offerings.

Personalize Pre-Launch Event

Throw your own "pre-launch" event where you can share your vision with friends, family, and other close supporters. This will give a complete overview of your product and company to your inner circle, who in turn will be more comfortable providing valuable introductions, endorsing the product, and empathizing with how busy you are during the campaign. This can be done one or two nights prior to your actual event. It can be done in your home or at a cool restaurant. This event won't be big, but will give the people closest to you the ability to see what all your hard work has resulted in!

Get Opinion Leaders On Board Early

The best way to do this is to set up a sponsored "influencer program" in which, in exchange for monetary compensation or free product, these influential bloggers will be sharing your story and event with their readers. Have them offer a giveaway so their readers are able to sample your product prior to launch. They can offer their readers a chance to win entrance to your party or appear on your company website.

Apple has a knack for getting thought leaders on board prior to their product launches. What has always set them apart is that they get the conversation started months before the product launches, usually before there's even a demo for anyone to see. No one is talking about what the product does; they're talking about what it might do.

Obviously, Apple's iconic stature helps. Journalists and bloggers know that Apple has a history of releasing innovative and useful products, and they bet on the fact that subsequent product releases would be just as innovative and useful. But this is a strategy anyone can use, even if they don't have a history and brand recognition like Apple.

No, you might not have the *New York Times* and CNN arguing about what your upcoming product is going to do, but you can start working with the media in advance of your product launch to get people talking, waiting, and wondering about what you are going to come up with. To do this, distribute your press release to a few select press outlets, as an "exclusive." Offer a sneak peek sample to editors and make sure these editors are aware of your launch event. Often startup launch events turn into full-scale parties because the right media outlets were able to promote it. Even if your efforts don't get you much coverage, you'll get something to build on. The media will know who you are, so come launch day at least you won't be starting cold, and that can make getting press a lot easier.

⋆⋆ Words of Wisdom from Fairy Godparents ⋆⋆

"Don't be intimidated by what you don't know. That can be your greatest strength and ensure that you do things differently from everyone else."

—Sara Blakely, founder of Spanx and world's youngest female billionaire

It is also a good idea to set up appointments with journalists prior to your launch. This gives you the opportunity to explain to them exactly what you are about in a more intimate environment. It will also give the editor ample time to sample your product and formulate any story ideas he or she may have.

Launch Day!

Finally! Your royal ball is here. On the day of the launch it is important to have your vendor info, a run of show (basically, an itinerary of exactly what will happen during the event), the guest list, and any other specifics immediately available to you on your tablet or smartphone, or in a well-organized binder. (Following, you'll see a sample run of show for one of our clients, PACT Baby.)

Always arrive plenty early to organize and make sure all the details are right. Make sure everyone working the event has your exact messaging down and is able to give your short business pitch as well as you are. For the event, anyone you have hired is part of your team and everything needs to run smoothly. Conduct yourself as a consummate calm professional regardless of what is happening. And of course, be ready to spread the word about your amazing idea with all the passion you have!

Run of Show Example—PACT Baby

Vendor Contacts:
List here: Names, affiliations, e-mail addresses, and telephone numbers

Date:
9 A.M.—Arrival of the Arieff Communications team for setup

9:30 A.M.—Florist to deliver flowers

10 A.M.—Arrival of food and DJ

11 A.M.—Arrival of guests. As editors arrive, Natalia to inform DJ of Spotify playlist

11:30 A.M.—Rosanne to talk about PACT, the new line and the manufacturing behind the organic cotton, why it is good for babies

12 P.M.—End of event

12:30 P.M.—Start cleanup and send comments, attendees, and any additional information back to PACT

KEY MESSAGES
Overall PACT Brand Messages:
★ PACT creates super-soft organic cotton apparel.
★ PACT is a cause-driven company.
★ Each season, PACT designs a new collection of clothing inspired by someone doing something good or by a cause. The collection not only benefits the cause but the designs are also inspired by the cause.

- ★ With every purchase, you help PACT make a positive change in our world.
- ★ PACT motto: You change your underwear. Together, we change the world.

Fall/Winter Key Messages:
- ★ PACT has partnered with the Whole Planet Foundation to help fund 100 new businesses around the world. The foundation will use the money raised by PACT for microloans to entrepreneurs in low-income communities.

Make a List and Check It Twice

To help you create your own master list, following is an example of the planning template that Adrienne's consumer and lifestyle public relations firm, Arieff Communications (*www.arieff.com*), uses for launches.

Cinderella's Pre-Launch Master List

Weeks 1 & 2:
- ★ Develop event theme (if wanted)
- ★ Finalize media list for event
- ★ Draft press release
- ★ Coordinate quotes from vendors for event—confirm vendors/quantities/logistics from photographer/caterer/valet/DJ
- ★ Determine media gift bags and incentives for bloggers
- ★ Recruit bloggers and/or set up a sponsored blogger program for pre and post event—bloggers to potentially hold giveaways

Week 3:
- ★ Finalize all event setup details
- ★ Send invites to media/influencers who cover a range of topics
- ★ Send out press release
- ★ Finalize RSVP list
- ★ Set up media/influencer VIP appointments

Week 4:

★ Last round of followups to confirm attendance

Week 5:

★ Deploy press release announcing new store opening
★ Arrange plans for your social media channels to actively interact with guests during and after the event

Week 6:

★ Send out post-event press release to local and/or national media regarding event attendees

⋆⋆ Chapter 6's Cinderella Principles ⋆⋆

Create a party that suits your purpose: Make the event represent you and your brand.

Match your party to your pocketbook: Be realistic about what you have to spend and what you can achieve with that.

Location, location, location: Think outside of the box to match your brand and your venue.

With a little help from your friends: Ask your friends to participate in spreading the word.

Creating a royal guest list: Invite the appropriate crowd, keep track of your guests, and use social media to promote your event.

It's the little things: Sneak in creative details that guests will remember.

Don't forget the bar! A signature cocktail or mocktail is a great idea.

Say it with swag: Prepare a little gift to say "thanks!"

Timing is everything: Give yourself enough time to prepare.

Make a list and check it twice: Think carefully about what you want to accomplish during your event.

Use the Pre-Launch Master List: Stay organized!

Start spreading the news: Use ongoing publicity and other promotional methods.

Stay in contact with contributors before, during, and after launch: Keep them updated about company changes and new products or services.

CHAPTER 7

Keep Your Eye on the Crown

★

STAY FOCUSED

*T*he king's son led her to the most honorable seat, and afterwards took her out to dance with him. She danced so very gracefully that they all more and more admired her. A fine meal was served up, but the young prince ate not a morsel, so intently was he busied in gazing on her.

She went and sat down by her sisters, showing them a thousand civilities, giving them part of the oranges and citrons which the prince had presented her with, which very much surprised them, for they did not know her. While Cinderella was thus amusing her sisters, she heard the clock strike eleven and three-quarters, whereupon she immediately made a courtesy to the company and hurried away as fast as she could.

Arriving home, she ran to seek out her godmother, and, after having thanked her, she said she could not but heartily wish she might go to the ball the next day as well . . .

Wowing at the Ball . . . Twice?

In today's popular version of the story, Cinderella goes to the ball only once and her fate is sealed. In fact, in most of the versions of the original fairy tale, Cinderella goes to the ball *twice*. This is an important distinction because it reminds us all that you can't just do something fabulous once and expect your life to change; you have to be able to do the same thing just as well, over and over again. Every royal adventure requires patience, consistency, repetition, and focus.

Cinderella and her fairy godmother had to pull off the whole ornate scheme, down to the pumpkin carriage and the shimmering ball gown and the glass slippers, twice. It is at the second ball that Cinderella wins the prince's heart, only to lose focus in the eleventh hour and nearly kill the deal.

When you're in the middle of the chaos and excitement of your first launch into the marketplace, and maybe have even been lucky enough to become a flavor of the moment that everybody wants to know, you have to remember to keep your eye on the crown. Resist getting carried away in the spirit of the moment, stay focused, and think long-term. Because this is not the last time you are going to have to go to the ball. So commit your energy and your resources in a way that is going to bring about lasting success, and don't get so wrapped up in the party that the clock strikes twelve.

⋆⋆ Words of Wisdom from Fairy Godparents ⋆⋆

"Do one thing every day that scares you."

—Eleanor Roosevelt, First Lady of the United States, 1933–1945

After all, in the story, once Cinderella gets the kingdom buzzing, she has to keep her momentum going so the prince is moved to throw another ball. Then she must summon her resources and her creativity once more, utilizing all of her newfound skills in order to keep putting herself back in the place where magic can happen.

Once you've had your business launch and made a big splash, one of the most important things you can do is build on that buzz and keep the excitement going. Here are some buzz-management tips that will help ensure you get asked back to the party.

Post-Launch Social Media Strategies

Social media is an invaluable tool for keeping the party going long after all your guests have gone home. Each social media tool offers you a different way to help your guests remember the great time they had and look forward to future events. It's also a great way to build a bigger guest list, by showing people who weren't there what they missed and encouraging them to be included the next time. Twitter, Facebook, YouTube, Pinterest, Instagram, and Tumblr are all fantastic tools for keeping the buzz buzzing. Here are some specific strategies you can try to keep the buzz buzzing!

Use Metrics to Your Advantage

Chart your progress regularly. Keep track of how many follows, likes, comments, and subscriptions you are getting and make the most of that information. Do more of what's working and pull back on what's not. Google and Facebook analytics provide some excellent (free!) information about the engagement level of your brand, and can help you adjust to make the most of the traffic you are receiving.

Use Relevant Hashtags and Tags

Hashtags and tags are a great way to make sure that your social media posts connect with the people who would be most interested in your brand. Hashtags, in particular, connect you to celebrities, influencers, thought leaders, and institutions as well as their large followings because you will show up in their feed. Similarly, tagging people in photos and comments that relate to them instantly gives you access to their social media followings, because you will show up on their wall.

Using hashtags while they're trending is a great way to ensure that your posts will reach a large amount of people. For example, if you were posting about the 2014 Sochi Olympics, which many referred to as "The Social Olympics," using the hashtag #sochi2014 would have entered you into a larger conversation which people were actively reading.

Reaching Celebrities

The best way to reach out to celebrities, influencers, and bloggers is to do your homework! This is one of those tips that everyone knows and nobody does. Reach out to a celebrity's handler before sending him or her a package. Random packages are never welcome, so make sure yours isn't random. Sites like WhoRepresents.com can help you find out how to get in touch with celebrities' managers or publicists.

When you reach out, you need to be really specific as to why you're reaching out. For example, if you have a T-shirt company, research which bloggers, celebrities, and influencers like T-shirts and then put together a short list.

The best way to reach out is still to send e-mails and place calls to their representatives, institutions, or agents with a pitch that clearly explains the goals of the campaign and why that particular celebrity is a great fit. Once you have had a positive response, encourage them to use their social channels and get the word out!

Here's an example. Our client AWAKE Chocolate ran a campaign with *The Bachelor* reality star Arie Luyendyk Jr. (*www.imdb.com/name/nm2085672/*), to target our audience of college-aged students and young adults in their twenties. We created a calendar of tweets, Facebook posts, and Instagram videos that aligned with the AWAKE Chocolate (*www.awakechocolate.com*) brand. On New Year's Eve, Arie Instagrammed and tweeted, "Double dose of caffeine? Tonight could get wild if I keep this up! @awakechocolate #NYE," and included a photo of him eating an AWAKE Chocolate bar.

Don't Oversell

People frequent social media destinations because they want to be informed, engaged, and entertained by the brands that they follow. They do not always want to be sold things. So make sure that your posts are something that is of interest to your readers. Offer them value, and a reward for stopping by. Just posting images of your product is a big turnoff. Here are some ways to use social media judiciously—so you encourage interaction without overselling.

★ Give a behind-the-scenes glimpse of your business operations.

★ Offer promo codes.

★ Launch a contest that encourages your fans to share images that are related to your brand with a dedicated hashtag.

★ If you're traveling, whether for work or pleasure, use that experience to add interesting content to your social media feeds. The Blonde Salad has a great fashion and travel Instagram (*www.instagram.com/chiaraferragni*); she stays on brand while traveling for work without promoting her clothing line in every post by using hashtags like #TheBlondeSaladGoesTo . . . and #TheBlondeSaladNeverStops.

★ Create fun content to share, such as videos and playlists that are available for download. Keep them on brand without shamelessly selling your product.

These tactics will help keep your customers coming back for more.

Keep Your Content Fresh

Once you start to build a social media following, you have to post frequently and regularly on all of your channels. The pace of social media is speeding up the cultural attention span overall, and the worst thing you can do is let your page get stale, let alone static. You want to encourage people to come back to your page often, and when they do, they should find new features and posts of interest in addition to an archive of older material that they can search and reference on demand. You should be updating Twitter every day. Since it's constantly updating, you can easily get lost in the Twitter world. Facebook should be updated two to three times per week. It is the most archived site, so your content is never lost, and how many times have you unfriended someone because they post too much? Instagram should be refreshed two to three times per week at the least. Your website or blog should be updated once per week.

Enlist the Help of Your Colleagues

Engage the communities of everyone who works with and for you in helping to manage the buzz by asking them to list your company on their social media profiles and to promote your successes through their personal channels.

Form Partnerships

Target complementary (not competing) businesses, groups, and organizations, and explore ways to help each other out on social media. Be a giver, not a taker. Cross-promote with other businesses, but don't copy posts. Always put your spin on things and add value, rather than reusing what is already there. This is how you start a dialogue that will grow over time with these constituencies. An example of a great partnership is MAC Cosmetics and Lady Gaga. Without stepping on each other's toes, they were able to successfully promote the new MAC line to Lady Gaga's 3.5 million followers, as well as to MAC's own million followers.

⋆ ⋆ Words of Wisdom from Fairy Godparents ⋆ ⋆

"I used to walk down the street like I was a superstar . . . I want people to walk around delusional about how great they can be—and then to fight so hard for it every day that the lie becomes the truth."

—Lady Gaga, singer-songwriter

Attend to the "Bad" as Well as the "Good"

Be sure to respond to customer concerns in a timely, private manner to address questions and solve problems. This offers you an opportunity to avoid any bad reviews, and also builds a reputation for your company as a caring, conscientious, and responsive brand. Sometimes the biggest complainers can turn out to be your most loyal customers, once you win them over. Responding to members of your brand community who have taken the time to reach out to you, even if they are a little disgruntled, is an opportunity to start a conversation that could last a lifetime. See Chapter 8 for more on dealing with a public relations crisis.

Cultivate Brand Evangelism

People who spread the word about Cinderella were more than just casual observers. People felt strongly about Cinderella, felt that something different had happened in their lives as a consequence of seeing her, and felt obliged to share the news with their friends. This is what is known as brand evangelism.

As we have learned from such companies as Apple, Red Bull, and Starbucks—to name just a few—brand evangelism is one of the most effective forms of advertising, and it's absolutely free. Social media is a great way to inspire brand evangelism and get people who have become disciples of your brand to spread the word about your company. Connecting yourself with a higher cause, giving back portions of your profits to a particular charity, and co-creating with your customers by responding to their requests and feedback are all excellent ways to build brand loyalty and get your community of customers inspired to spread the good news.

Evangelism Starts at Home

Brand evangelism starts with integrity and integrity begins with the way you deal with your business family. Your employees (if you have any yet) are, generally speaking, the ones who create a first impression about your brand. If your employees (or you!) are unhappy, uninvolved, or uneducated about the business, and unenthusiastic about what they are doing, this will be communicated to your customers. Treating your people well, and thus building a passionate and committed community that begins at home, is the first and most important step toward expanding your tribe beyond your immediate brand family.

⋅Words of Wisdom from Fairy Godparents⋅

"I've learned that people will forget what you said, people will forget what you did, but people will never forget how you made them feel."

—Maya Angelou, author and poet

Your Brand Should Add Real Value to People's Lives

If you want to develop a community of brand evangelists as opposed to just customers, then people not only need to endorse you, or buy from you, they have to rave about you to their network. In order to inspire this kind of enthusiasm in your brand community, you have to provide them with products and services that add real value, and in some way change life—whether in a big or small way—as a result of interacting with your brand.

You can make your employees and customers feel that they are part of a community of people who are giving back with their consumer dollars, as TOMS Shoes and Raintees do. Or you can provide a first-time-ever experience for your customers that revolutionizes the way they experience media, the way Apple did. For your customers and employees to become brand evangelists, you need to make them feel that your brand is meaningful and your product helps them be a part of something bigger than themselves.

CINDERELLA CEO PROFILE

Beth Doane
Raintees
www.raintees.com

"We can solve our world's greatest humanitarian and environmental issues by giving every time we buy."

—Beth Doane

According to *www.raintees.com*, "Beth was 22 when she founded her first company, launching exclusive European fashion labels across the United States. What she didn't expect was to discover horrific human rights violations, environmental pollution, and child labor throughout the industry. Determined to show that fashion could be produced ethically, without harming people or the planet, Beth created Raintees in

2008." For every Raintee sold, the company plants a tree in a rainfor-est. Raintees also donates school supplies to a child in need for every totebag they sell.

As stated on *www.raintees.com*, "Beth's remarkable journey from fashion runways to saving rainforests has captivated audiences at TEDx, the United Nations, Google, and the National Mall in Wash-ington, D.C., where she has spoken about the power of giving back and creating social change. Beth has also been featured in *National Geographic*, *Glamour*, *InStyle*, and other publications. She is also the founder of Andira Creative, a consulting and design firm based in Los Angeles."

Tell a Compelling Brand Story

People love a great story, and living and communicating a compelling and acces-sible brand narrative that resonates with your community is a great way to build an evangelical base. Here is a list of the elements that most great brand stories include:

The Elements of a Great Brand Story

★ Offers human and heroic stories about the brand founders
★ Shows that the stakes are higher than just the success of the company
★ Makes customers feel that they are an integral part of the brand story
★ Encourages the brand community to engage and converse with each other about the story
★ Innovates ways to link profit with purpose
★ Rewards brand evangelism and brand loyalty

Branding Is Strategic

When Cinderella goes to the ball for the second time, she makes sure to stay true to her brand and her brand message. In this way, she reinforces the impression she made the first time and takes it a step further. This establishes brand consistency, and a brand promise. While marketing may contribute to a brand, the brand is big-ger than any particular marketing effort. The brand is what remains after the marketing has swept through the room. It's what sticks in your mind associated with a product, service, or organization—whether or not, at that particular moment, you bought it. So be sure, especially in the beginning, to keep your brand consistent each and every time.

The brand and brand consistency is ultimately what determines whether you will win a loyal customer base. The marketing may convince you to buy a particular BMW, and maybe it's the first foreign car you ever owned, but it is the brand that will determine if you will only buy BMWs for the rest of your life.

A brand is built from many things. Very important among these things is the lived experience of the brand. Did that car deliver on its brand promise of reliability? Did the maker continue to uphold the quality standards that made them what they are? Did the salesperson and the service center mechanic know what they were talking about? Branding makes loyal customers, advocates, and evangelists.

BENEFICENT BRAND: WHOLE FOODS

What the Whole Foods story teaches us is that the most important element in any business is the people. It is through understanding this that a couple of health-conscious businessmen took the natural foods industry by storm. Without the loyal support and help of thousands of its consumers, Whole Foods would never have reached the point of success they're experiencing today.

Whole Foods proudly lists their core values on its website, in marketing materials, and in stores, and the unifying element of each of these is *people*:

Whole Foods Market's Core Values
★ Selling the highest-quality natural and organic products available
★ Satisfying and delighting our customers
★ Supporting team member excellence and happiness
★ Creating wealth through profits and growth
★ Caring about our communities and our environment
★ Creating ongoing win-win partnerships with our suppliers
★ Promoting the health of our stakeholders through healthy eating education

It Takes a Village

Creating an environment where people feel a part of a community that is connected through the brand is another crucial element of brand evangelism. In today's socialized culture, building connections and relationships with your community and helping them to do the same thing with each other is crucial. If people come to feel a part of a brand community that they identify with and rely upon in their daily lives, they will be brand advocates for life.

✦ Words of Wisdom from Fairy Godparents ✦

"Passion is energy. Feel the power that comes from focusing on what excites you."

—Oprah Winfrey, entrepreneur and personality

Provide Your Customers with a Great Experience Every Time

This may sound old-fashioned, but the very best way to build passionate and committed brand followers is to give them a memorable and pleasurable brand experience each and every time they interact with your website, your store, or your product. This means that every step of the way in the interaction should be simple, transparent, pleasant, and concerned first and foremost with customer care and satisfaction. You are not just selling a product anymore; you are selling an experience that people should want to repeat over and over again.

Reward Brand Advocacy

There are many ways that you can build into your business model that reward people for becoming brand advocates. Contests for the best or most unusual use of your product, or for the best commercial featuring their reviews of your product, can be rewarded with inner circle membership, prizes, or discounts—just some of the ways that you can incentivize people to get involved and spread the world. Dogfish Head Ale has never had to make a commercial because their brand advocates make their own commercials and compete for inclusion in the Dogfish Head elite community who get to decide which rare and bespoke ale will be brewed up next. Pinpointing the passionate evangelists in your community and beginning a relationship with them that encourages them to keep spreading the word far and wide is an inexpensive and long-term approach to building an evergreen and ever-expanding brand community.

CINDERELLA CEO PROFILE

Brit Morin
Brit + Co.
www.brit.co

> *"The home is the center of our lives. It can and should be a more creative, functional, and beautiful place for us to spend our time."*

—Brit Morin

Brit Morin is the founder and CEO of Brit + Co., an online platform and e-commerce company that encourages the digital generation to create. She's also a mom, a journalist, and a news correspondent—pretty impressive, huh? In late 2012, the team launched their first foray into commerce, with DIY Kits of projects featured on Brit.co. Each kit contains everything you need to make your favorite Brit + Co. projects in sixty minutes or fewer. In 2014, Brit opened her first brick and mortar store in San Francisco. Modeled like a country cottage in the middle of a city, Brit's MakeShop has drawn the attention of the *New York Times* and many other news outlets. Brit + Co. has partnered with influential companies like Pinterest, Intel, Fab, L'Oreal, YouTube, UNIQLO, Alloy Media, 3M, Nikon, and Brit has been featured in publications like the *Los Angeles Times*, *Huffington Post*, *People*, *Lucky*, *Forbes*, *Parade*, *USA Today*, and *Fortune*. She is a regular DIY/lifestyle correspondent on *The Today Show* and was the featured tech correspondent for Katie Couric's daytime talk show, *Katie*, nationally syndicated on ABC.

As Britt says on *www.brit.co*, "It wasn't until after I left my job at Google that I had time to finally learn how to perform domestic skills the proper way. But I still found that many of the popular things to make, whether in the kitchen or at the craft table, were very complicated and took hours to perfect. And if most people are like me, I know that as much as they want to be creative, they won't complete a project or attempt a recipe if it's too difficult or takes too much time, especially given how little time we have in our lives these days. Thus, I made it my new mission to use what I learned from my life in technology to find and create innovative hacks for making beautiful things in and around the home, whether that means an app that will do all your grocery shopping for you, or a simpler recipe for your next dinner party. By continuing to keep my finger on the pulse of technology, I'm also able to scour the web for innovative websites, apps, and software that also aide us in leading a better life in and around the home. This website is the nesting place for all these things; it is a collection of me and my team's handpicked and handmade ideas for creative living."

Plan and Provide for Controlled Business Growth

Launching a business is a very different process from maintaining and growing a business. Now that you've launched your business, you will need a new business plan that provides for controlled business growth. Grow too quickly and you run the risk of burning yourself out or tapping a demand that you cannot supply. This can be as fatal to a new business as not selling a single unit of anything.

The idea now is to set realistic goals that you can reach while growing at a brisk but steady and sustainable pace. You need a growth plan that allows you to put down solid roots that will develop over time and sink deep into the earth, rather than long thin roots that cling to the surface and can be swept away by the first winds of trend change.

Here are some things that you can do to control and manage your growth, rather than letting your growth control and manage you!

Communicate with Your Vendors and Partners

Make sure that you keep your business partners, vendors, and suppliers updated on your growth expectations so that they too can plan for and adapt to the demand. Remember, they are growing with you!

★ Contact them about finding lower rates on materials.
★ Ask if they have any ideas on how to speed up production and shipping.
★ Ask if they're able to keep up with your demand.
★ Make sure all are looped into the financial expectations.

Set New Goals

Setting reasonably high, but specific, goals will increase performance and motivation, even if you don't end up reaching the goal. If you set goals that are too easy to reach, then you won't be incented to push harder and jump higher. If you set your goals too high, however, you run the risk of exhausting and discouraging yourself and your staff.

So keep raising the bar, and be ambitious, but also be judicious—and don't forget to maintain a work-life balance for yourself and your staff in the process. It's helpful to prioritize a few goals at a time so that you don't get overwhelmed and can maintain surgical focus in the areas you want to grow, expand, or improve.

Here are some examples of goals that might work (with some specificity added) for your company:

★ Increase sales by 10 percent in our second year.
★ Reduce delivery time by one week.
★ Optimize website to make consumer shopping easier.
★ Research and source additional recycled materials for products.

Create new goals like these each year to keep yourself and your staff focused and motivated. Check in with your goals every few months to see how you're doing, and be sure you stay on track. At the end of each year, assess your progress and celebrate goals you've achieved with everyone who contributed. If you missed the mark on some goals, ask yourself why. Was the timeline too short? Did the market change mid-year? Rewrite the goal if necessary and shoot for it again next year.

Allocate Resources

Your money is precious—so treat it that way. It is among your most valuable growth resources, and you need to guard it carefully. Just because you have the money doesn't mean you need to spend it now; save up for a future, larger investment that could benefit your business in the long run, or keep it as a cushion to fall back on during a slow period. Your time is also very precious, so prioritize tasks, don't waste energy on unnecessary effort, and delegate if necessary. For example, if your support team is able to take over letting the media know about a new product your company is launching, let them send e-mails and make calls. Use the time you freed up to see the media representative in person and create long-standing relationships.

Make New Friends but Keep the Old

When you are in a growth spurt and are making and finding new relationships and communities, it can be easy to forget who brought you to the ball. Don't forget about your existing customers—even though it is exciting that you've attracted new customers, make sure existing customers receive the same or better level of service. New friends are silver, but old friends are pure gold. Treat them that way.

Consider Your Staff

Think about whether or not the growth that you expect will require hiring staff, or adding new positions or support personnel to the staff that you have already engaged. Now that you are growing as a business, you may need to grow your staff as well, so be observant and notice where things are falling through the cracks, and where you might benefit from adding to your work force.

This may also be a good time to fire up the staff who currently supports you. You can maximize the human resources that you already have by inspiring and instilling them with the same passion for growth and success that you are feeling. Make sure everyone is on the same page by holding weekly planning and metric-setting/evaluation meetings. You can use this time to discuss and set new goals.

Assembling Your Royal Entourage

Learning how to recognize, hire, and build a relationship with key personnel is crucial to the long-term success of any business. Having the right people in the right positions earning the right compensation is a tricky balance, and it begins with learning how to recognize who is a valuable employee and who is perhaps better off in another position, or a different company.

Here are some telltale signs that you are talking to people who should become a part of your inner circle:

* **They display loyalty:** These employees always seek to do the right things. They are mindful of the company's long-term goals, not their own personal goals. They will always be willing to steer you in the right direction, whether you agree with it or not.

* **They praise their peers:** Truly loyal employees care: about the company, about its customers, about its mission . . . they feel they're working for something greater than just themselves. So they appreciate when another employee does something great because that means the company is fulfilling its mission. Employees that praise and recognize others, especially when it's not their job to do so, display great interpersonal skills. (When you do some-thing well, praise from your boss feels great . . . but it's also, at least generally speaking, expected. At least it should be. Praise from a peer feels awesome, especially when you respect that person.)

* **They disagree when necessary:** Though it may be difficult to appreciate at the time, you want to work with people who are not afraid to disagree with you or with the company's plans. Loyal employees who disagree—but always keep the company's values and mission in mind—are a valuable asset.

* **They support the company's decisions:** After a decision is made, loyal employees get behind that decision. And they don't just pay the decision lip service; they really work hard toward achieving that goal.

* **Unfortunately, they might quit:** Since loyal employees are often your best employees, the last thing you want is for them to leave. These great employees often help you re-hire and train their own replacements, though.

Where Can You Find Great Employees?

At large companies such as Apple, there's a constant influx of resumes and people desperate to get their foot in the door for an opportunity at such an innovative large company. But for early-stage startups, resources are usually tight. Most great candidates have never even heard of you, so it's hard to trade on prestige and get a full boat of interns working for you just because they are dying to be at your company.

Fortunately, there are people who (like you) thrive on uncertainty. They value equity and ownership over salary and stability. How do you find these people? Personal networks! Yes, social media comes into play in just about all aspects of our professional and personal lives these days—even hiring.

Other great tactics for hiring people in startup culture include:

* Hiring people under part-time status is an option if you can't afford them full-time; they can then consult with other businesses to make extra money.
* Be clear about your company's environment. It's very important to make sure that whoever you hire has the right chemistry for you, the other people associated with the business, and the brand you are launching.
* Be transparent in what you can offer at the beginning. Have everything in writing in the form of an employee contract. You can find sample employee contracts in a Google search and tweak them to fit your company culture.

Establish a Good Company Culture

Almost every startup company starts off "scrappy," and there's a well-established tendency in the tech startup scene to embrace the cheap mentality.

We have seen this problem up close so many times. You have an early-stage company that had originally raised $100,000 and then later raises $5 million but still acts like a seed-stage startup. Your first year is going to be lean, sure. But if all is going well, you can become less lean in terms of a nicer office, salary, benefits, and perks. That is stage 2! A great office environment is important, as you are spending five days a week there, and sometimes a lot more than that.

A great office helps with productivity and output. It helps with employee retention. You don't have to spend a fortune, but do realize that as you grow you should budget accordingly.

Good Employees Are Not Replaceable

When a company loses a great employee, it's natural for other employees to think about greener pastures as well. You can retain your employees by creating a good work culture for them, making sure their work environment is comfortable and positive, and creating a space that is productive but fun. Also give your employees the opportunity to move up and take on new responsibilities. Growth potential is a huge incentive to stay with a company.

At the end of the day, it won't be a great product or service or technology that makes a company succeed—it will be the great people who work there. Treat everyone well—always, especially your valued staff members.

Royal Role Model Q&A

 **Amy Zhang**

Tell us a little about your background.

My name is Amy Zhang, and I'm a fourth-year Electrical Engineering and Computer Science (EECS) major at UC Berkeley. My career in STEM (science, technology, engineering, and math) started at an early age with a love for math, science, and Legos, and came to fruition through FIRST Robotics. I came to Berkeley as Engineering Undeclared but eventually settled in EECS after hearing a very enthusiastic professor speak about his passion in computer science. Upon arrival at college, I joined the Society of Women Engineers as a freshman and am now the president of my collegiate section. After graduation, I plan on working at Google as a software engineer.

What is a hobby you enjoy and how has it helped you with confidence?

The theater bug bit me a long time ago. I have always loved storytelling, acting, and the imagination that comes along with a good play or musical. At Berkeley, I am also a Theater and Performance Studies minor. I did a little bit of theater back in middle school and in college have taken two acting classes. Although my engineering classes make it difficult to find time to participate in productions, these acting classes have given me the courage to not care so much about what other people think and to know it's okay to be silly sometimes. In order to become another character, you first have to gain a deep understanding of yourself. You have to come fully into your mind and body before you can truly take on the form of another. Acting has given me a greater understanding of myself and of my fears, which in turn brings me that much closer to conquering them.

Who was your favorite professor and why?

I don't know if he was my favorite professor, but he was definitely one of the most influential. His name is Professor Paul Hilfinger and I had him for data structures at UC Berkeley. It was perhaps one of the most difficult classes I've gone through, but it was also one that I learned the most in. Not only did I learn how to program (and to program well) but Professor Hilfinger is one of the most dedicated professors I have ever met. When we were up at 4 A.M. trying to make our project work, he was up with us at 4 A.M. answering all of our questions. Even still, he was an intimidating professor who rarely tolerated incompetence. However, he taught me how to fend for myself, and also how to ask for help when you need it. He taught me to do my research so I can ask smart and productive questions. And the crazy thing is he will do that for *all* of his students, as long as they take the initiative to show they care. He may not even remember who I am, but I will always remember what a great professor he is.

Do you have any words of wisdom to share with young entrepreneurs?

Learn to live a little. We all have goals, dreams, and ambitions. It's important that you take the time to find out what you want and do what you love. The beauty about not knowing what you want to do with the rest of your life is that you have the rest of your life to figure it out. Just remember not to get too caught up in the big picture because you want to be able to live in the present and enjoy life's special little moments.

Remember to not let other people tell you what you can or can't do. As Steve Jobs said in his Stanford graduation speech, "Your time is limited so don't waste it living someone else's life." But you should make sure that you actually do live yours.

⋆ Chapter 7's Cinderella Principles ⋆

Post-launch social media strategies: Use hashtags and tags, fresh content, and new partnerships to attend to both good and bad online situations.

Cultivate brand evangelism: Add value to people's lives so they want to tell your story.

Provide customers with a great experience and reward brand advocacy: This is how you maintain a happy customer base.

Plan and provide for controlled business growth: Set new goals, allocate resources, make new customers but keep old ones happy, consider your staff, and assemble your entourage to support and inspire you.

When the Clock Strikes Twelve, Don't Panic

★

DEAL WITH OBSTACLES

The next day the two sisters were at the ball, and so was Cinderella, but dressed even more magnificently than before. The king's son was always by her, and never ceased his compliments and kind speeches to her. All this was so far from being tiresome to her, and, indeed, she quite forgot what her godmother had told her. She thought that it was no later than eleven when she counted the clock striking twelve. She jumped up and fled, as nimble as a deer. The prince followed, but could not overtake her. She left behind one of her glass slippers, which the prince picked up most carefully.

Communications Fundamentals for Cinderellas in Crisis

When Cinderella forgets her fairy godmother's instructions and overstays her curfew, she doesn't panic or freeze. Instead, she springs into motion, removing herself from the situation as quickly as she can, so she doesn't undo her entire campaign before it even gets started. Ironically, it is the splash that she makes leaving the ball so suddenly, and the glass slipper she accidentally leaves behind, that give the prince the tools he needs to later find Cinderella.

Even in a fairy-tale world, despite your best intentions, things will go wrong. You'll find yourself in the middle of a disaster and having to think fast and do some fancy footwork, even though you're wearing glass slippers. What Cinderella discovers is that sometimes a sudden change or unexpected development is exactly what is needed to innovate your way to new levels of success.

When unforeseen events conspire to create a crisis or catastrophe, it gives you this opportunity to explore new avenues to your desired goal that may never have otherwise emerged. Failure, even a seemingly large one, might just be the glass slipper that makes your dream come true in the end.

As in any crisis, communication is the key to a successful resolution. Crisis communications at its most basic level consists of three phases:

★ Disaster preparedness
★ Crisis response
★ Crisis recovery

Let's take a closer look at each phase, so you can come out of any crisis as successfully as Cinderella did.

Phase 1: Disaster Preparedness

The best way to handle a crisis is to be prepared for one in the first place. Change is a constant, and you will hit a few bumps in the road along the way no matter how well you navigate. Building this philosophy into your business model from the onset will ensure that you and your staff have the agility and the responsiveness you will need to respond to a crisis when the need arises.

Creating a disaster preparedness plan means that you will have the tools right at your fingertips to respond quickly, strategically, and responsibly when sudden change or catastrophe strikes. Just like knowing where your emergency exits and fire extinguishers are before there is a fire, having a plan in place before crisis strikes maximizes your chances of survival with minimal damage, and gives you the greatest potential for turning a short-term failure into a long-term success.

✦ Words of Wisdom from Fairy Godparents ✦

"As a leader, I am tough on myself and I raise the standard for everybody; however, I am very caring because I want people to excel at what they are doing so that they can aspire to be me in the future."

—Indra Nooyi, CEO of PepsiCo

Here are some steps to consider when you are putting together your disaster preparedness plan so you are ready when (and not if) a crisis occurs.

Disaster Preparedness Plan for Princesses in a Pickle

1. **Define what constitutes a crisis for your business:** Think about all of the ways that your business is vulnerable and what constitutes a crisis for you. Is it business suddenly drying up? A cash flow shortage? A faulty product? A run of bad press? Lots of negative feedback on social media? A sudden spike in the cost of your materials? A competing product hitting the marketplace? Consider all of the areas in which your business might be vulnerable and then imagine ways to guard against crises, or ways to manage and innovate around it if the worst happens.

2. **Assign responsibilities:** Once you have thought through your potential risks and the probable responses to each of them, take a look at your staff and figure out who is going to do what when a crisis hits. When you are in the throes of an emergency, the tendency is to just shout "all hands on deck" without thinking through who is going to be best at what task. That sort of chaos can also lead to miscommunication and overcommunication to the press. Thinking ahead about who is best suited to handle each step of your crisis management plan can prevent a lot of confusion once the wave hits.

3. **Appoint a spokesperson:** Whether it's you, someone else in your organization, or someone you hire from the outside, make sure that the person you have in place has some media training and knows how to explain, in a transparent and forward-looking fashion, what steps your business is taking to remedy the situation. It is also a good idea to prepare statements and materials for each potential crisis you have identified in your plan so that you have materials and a position ready at a moment's notice.

4. **Be ready to use all the social media tools available to communicate:** Get your message across on Twitter, Facebook, Instagram, your blog, and any other platform you have for your business. It would even be worthwhile to post a video of yourself giving real-time updates or a heartfelt apology on YouTube or Facebook.

5. **Apologize early! Then say sorry again:** Offer generous givebacks right away if that's appropriate for the situation. Your customers will know that you value them.

6. **Practice your plan:** Stage some business catastrophe fire drills and see if your plan works. This can be tailored for a small or large company; a "catastrophe" can mean a lot of different things, from a malfunctioning product to a not-so well spoken CEO. Going through the motions in advance will help you shore up holes in your plan, and will give everybody involved a working knowledge of what their responsibilities will be in the event of a crisis. This minimizes mistakes and missteps in the heat of the moment.

GREAT COMEBACKS: JET BLUE AND CHOBANI

Here are two great examples of companies who ran into a crisis and successfully handled it.

JetBlue

The Crisis: JetBlue's operations collapsed after an ice storm hit the East Coast of the United States, leading to 1,000 cancelled flights in just five days. JetBlue waited as long as possible to cancel flights, but that left a lot of people in the lurch. Some passengers were stuck on planes for hours on end.

The Crisis Response: CEO David Neeleman never blamed the weather. He wrote a public letter of apology to customers, introduced a customer's bill of rights, and presented monetary compensation for customers as well as what the company would do to help all the affected passengers.

The Crisis Recovery: JetBlue managed to quash much of the uproar by being as public and straightforward as possible. The CEO went on YouTube apologizing for his company's faults. Although there was much reputational damage done, JetBlue's comeback allowed it to regain some of its luster. They proved that they were about customer service even within the crisis.

Chobani

The Crisis: A quality issue with a small batch of its product. This led to an attack on their reputation on many different levels, especially with the growing influence of customer satisfaction and reviews. They had to immediately manage the situation before suffering permanent damage to an impressive company reputation.

The Crisis Response: Chobani acknowledged the problem immediately and was quick to post updates on its social media profiles as well as on its website. They allowed their customers to air their grievances across all platforms, because people want the opportunity to "get it out." Their CEO spoke about the issue, and they ceased all other promotions to let their customers know that their number one priority was getting the quality crisis under control.

The Crisis Recovery: The crisis resolved quickly, without any lasting impact to brand reputation or popularity. The crisis only served to strengthen their reputation as a brand that cares about the health and well-being of their customers first and foremost.

Phase 2: Crisis Response

Once a crisis has happened, you can't dive under the covers and hide until conditions improve. The key to successful crisis management is to respond, and quickly. This is why it's a good idea to have practiced your responses in advance.

The best posture for a business to take during a crisis is to be open and honest. Apologize if necessary and take responsibility where appropriate. Don't pass the buck, and don't deny the problem. Acknowledge the situation; meet the matter head on. If Cinderella had hung around after she realized that it was midnight, thinking "Oh the clock is wrong" or "What does that old fairy godmother know anyway; my carriage won't turn back into a pumpkin," instead of taking responsibility for her mistake and moving to mitigate the damage, the fairy tale might have had a very different ending.

·*· Words of Wisdom from Fairy Godparents ·*·

"If you are successful, it is because somewhere, sometime, someone gave you a life or an idea that started you in the right direction. Remember also that you are indebted to life until you help some less fortunate person, just as you were helped."

—Melinda Gates, philanthropist

The most important strategies are to be real, to be honest, to be fact-based, and to be humble. There are, however, some important rules to keep in mind in any crisis response effort; they will help get your message across in a way that moves toward resolve, rather than an escalation of the problem.

ROYAL ROLE MODEL

Samantha Garvey

While high school senior Samantha Garvey was hard at work on her research to preserve the mussel populations of Long Island, her family suddenly became homeless. Samantha didn't panic, but moved into the shelter with her family and continued her studies, which earned her a nomination in the Intel national science fair.

Once her impressive accomplishments began making headlines, donations and support from people across the country started pouring in. Although the aspiring marine biologist did not win the Intel competition, she was awarded a $50,000 scholarship and invited to attend the State of the Union address at the White House; her family was even given a new home in Bay Shore, Long Island. Samantha's example of grace under fire is a reminder of how courage in a time of crisis can lead to new and greater opportunities, support, and success.

What to Do When the Clock Strikes Twelve Checklist

1. **Don't panic!** When you find yourself in a crisis, it's best not to do the most instinctual thing and freak out. Remove yourself from the situation, take deep long breaths, and clear your head. No one ever solved a crisis by panicking and blurting out the first things that come to mind.
2. **Deal with people first in both your actions and your words.** Your relationships are the most valuable part of your growing business, so reach out to protect those assets first. If you put the needs of your people first, and put their best interests at the front of any response, the rest will follow much more easily, and you will have the best chance of recovering and even growing the true value of your business.
3. **Don't speculate.** No matter how sure you are about something, don't suggest that you know things that you may not. The worst way to respond

to a crisis is to create another one based on false information that you are presenting as truth. So know the facts and don't stray from them. Don't assume, or imagine, or believe, or guess, or wish. Only say things that you objectively know to be true, once you've gathered the facts and checked them twice.

4. **Avoid absolutes.** Words such as "always" and "never" have no place in crisis response, because you may live to regret them! Always leave yourself some wiggle room, particularly as the facts of the situation are still emerging. You may not know the whole story yet.

5. **Don't argue.** You should never engage in debate during a crisis. Arguing will only make the crisis escalate and create more drama among the parties involved.

6. **Shore up your allies.** Reach out to those with whom you have a positive relationship, since you may need to access this reservoir of goodwill you've established. Speak directly to your customers, suppliers, partners, and staff. Reestablish the connection that may have been shaken as a result of what's happened. In a crisis, more than at any other time, you need the support of your allies and friends.

7. **Stay organized.** Your organizational values are more important during a crisis than at any other time. Often crisis demands fast action, but in order to manage a crisis successfully you have to be methodical and take things one at a time. Set key messages and strategy; make an action list and follow it.

Crisis Management Cheat Sheet

★ Set key messages
★ Set specific objectives
★ Determine the metrics you'll use to assess your performance
★ Acknowledge mistakes, be transparent
★ Tailor messages to address the aggrieved or angry party
★ Note the other side's concerns; don't be dismissive

Cinderella's Secrets for How to Handle a Cyberscandal

While social media offers a whole new world of opportunities, alliances, and vital connections to small brands today, it can be a double-edged sword. In Generation Like, where the world is only a tweet away, nothing you say or do goes unnoticed as a brand. Today people can respond positively or negatively about your brand at turbo speed, and they will! If you go viral for a positive reason, you can become a household name overnight. Unfortunately, the same is true if you get caught at a less-than-stellar moment, when you are not at your royal best. While most of us won't wind up in the middle of a viral cyberscandal, it is important to remember that in a socialized world, you will at some point have to deal with cyber-risk. You will need to learn how to manage your brand's digital presence and steer your brand reputation safely through some occasionally rocky feedback.

⋆ Words of Wisdom from Fairy Godparents ⋆

"We need to accept that we won't always make the right decisions, that we'll screw up royally sometimes—understanding that failure is not the opposite of success, it's part of success."

—Arianna Huffington, editor-in-chief of *Huffington Post*

Here are some tips to keep in mind when you find yourself on the brink of a downward digital spiral.

★ **Make a cyber-response plan in advance:** Just as with any situation in crisis management, you are better off when you are prepared with a plan mapping out how you will respond in a cybercrisis. The best cyberdefense is a good cyberoffense. Think through your vulnerabilities. What problems might you be likely to face? Who on your team does what in a cybercrisis? Do you have each others' cell numbers so you can get in touch if something is starting to incinerate online? A plan is a valuable guide that you can follow when things heat up and you may not be able to be as calm and rational as you are now.

★ **Know when you've got a problem:** The quicker you recognize an issue, the greater opportunity you have for containing the problem and limiting the damage. So staying on top of your social media presence by monitoring it every day will ensure that when you start having a problem, you will be the first to know about it.

★ **Identify the source of the problem:** You can't respond to a crisis until you know the facts of the situation. The quickest way to get a handle on the facts is to figure out the root of the problem. Who or what is causing the problem? And why? Are they at fault, or are you? Only when you learn the actual facts of the situation can you rule appropriately and bring about a happy ending.

★ **Don't overreact:** Having a plan in place can also be a good guard against panicking and overreacting to the situation before you have learned what the facts are and been able to think through how your company wants to handle these situations. Seeming hysterical, or defensive, or argumentative, or overly apologetic will only add fuel to the fire. So when a crisis hits, behave like a queen: stay calm, learn the facts, consider your options, and only then react appropriately to the situation and reestablish peace in the kingdom.

★ **Get right back up on the horse:** Social media got you here, and social media will get you out. When something negative blows up about your brand and people are spreading less than love, responding properly to your detractors with professionalism, understanding, refreshing honesty, and a little dose of self-deprecating humor can literally save the day.

Here is an example of a good brand response that turned cyberscandal into cybersuccess and a better brand reputation.

SOCIAL MEDIA SCANDAL WINNER:
THE RED CROSS AND DOGFISH HEAD ALE

Here are two great examples of companies who ran into a crisis and successfully handled it.

The Crisis: Red Cross employee Gloria Huang accidentally tweeted the following on the official Red Cross Twitter page. The tweet stayed up for only an hour and still went viral.

Ryan found 2 more 4 bottle packs of Dogfish Head's Midas Touch Beer . . . when we drink we do it right #gettingslizzered

The Crisis Response: The Red Cross pulled down the tweet and tweeted the following:

We've deleted the rogue tweet but rest assured the Red Cross is sober and we've confiscated the keys.

The casual, forgiving, kind of funny, we're-all-human tone that the Red Cross adopted did more than just defuse the explosive potential danger to their brand reputation. They established a good-natured conversation with the viral traffic, and in doing so became a hipper, more culturally aware, and human brand.

Soon, even Dogfish Head Ale chimed in with this tweet:

Good plan! After I drop off a pint of blood @RedCross, I'm replacing it with a pint of @dogfishbeer #gettingslizzered

Dogfish Head Ale socialized the situation on their own Twitter and Facebook feeds, pushing the "donate a pint and drink a pint" campaign, and driving Red Cross donations nationwide, using the hashtag #gettingslizzered.

The Red Cross concluded the matter with these perfect parting words:

In the meantime we found so many of you to be sympathetic and understanding. While we're a 130 year old humanitarian organization, we're also made of up human beings. Thanks for not only getting that but for turning our faux pas into something good.

You immediately embraced this mix-up and many of you have pledged donations to the Red Cross.

SOCIAL MEDIA SCANDAL LOSER: APPLEBEE'S AND REDDITOR GALEFLAN

Here is an example of a bad brand response that made a cybermountain out of a molehill.

The Crisis: An excessively "thrifty" pastor refused to pay the 18 percent gratuity customarily charged by Applebee's for parties over eight. Instead, the pastor crossed out the tip, replacing it with a zero, and added the following deep thought scribbled over the signature on the charge slip:

"I give God 10 percent why do you get 18?"

Redditor Galeflan, AKA Chelsea, the Applebee's waitress who had just got stiffed, took a picture of the pastor's comment on the charge slip and posted it on Reddit with her own thoughts on the subject, saying:

"My mistake sir, I'm sure Jesus will pay for my rent and groceries."

The post went viral in four days. When the pastor called to complain, Applebee's fired Chelsea the waitress for a breach of privacy, which pushed the whole thing into the cyberscandal stratosphere of negative feedback. Tens of thousands began posting about the pastor's bad tip, and Applebee's bad attitude.

The Crisis Response: Instead of addressing their unhappy community's concerns, Applebee's chose to defend their actions. They argued with their site users' criticisms and posted disclaimers, without ever appearing to listen to their cybercommunity's feedback and take appropriate action to make the situation better. Of course, their defensive and combative response only fueled the fire, and the matter blew up into a viral scandal that damaged the Applebee brand.

ROYAL ROLE MODEL

Ruslana Lyzhychko
Pop-Star for Peace
www.ruslana.ua

> *"I am not afraid of your clubs, I am not afraid of your gas attacks! I am just a singer, singing songs for peace in Ukraine. If needed, I will sing every night in Maidan until next presidential election in 2015."*

—Ruslana

Originating from the Western Ukrainian city of L'viv, Ruslana began her musical career at the age of four. At seven, she went on tour with a children's ensemble, later graduating from the music conservatory in L'viv Ukraine as a pianist and a conductor. Over the next few years, Ruslana received more than forty awards within Ukraine, and broke out internationally, dominating charts throughout Europe and receiving the prestigious World Music Award in Las Vegas as the top-selling Ukrainian artist in the world.

In November 2013, when Ukrainian citizens rallied peacefully against their government, Ruslana stepped into the fray. Despite death threats and hostile police, she performed the Ukrainian national anthem nearly every night for three months, playing performances up to ten hours long each to keep the protestors' spirits up. One freezing night in December, as armed security forces descended on the square, Ruslana remained onstage, encouraging the activists to stand their ground and resist nonviolently.

As a result of Ruslana's courage in the face of crisis, she is now known around the world as the voice of her people, campaigning for peace in an increasingly dangerous region. Ruslana was named one of the most influential women of 2013 by *Forbes* magazine, and is the recipient of the 2014 Woman of Courage Award, which she received from Michelle Obama.

Phase 3: Crisis Recovery

When Cinderella suddenly found that she had overshot her curfew, she has to come up with a plan B quickly, lest her carriage turn back into a pumpkin before she returned home. Your business's crisis recovery involves making some changes too, sometimes right in the midst of the moment. Change is a necessary skill for any organization that wants to survive over the long haul. Crisis recovery is an opportunity to learn new lessons about your business, to apply what you have learned in the aftermath, and to grow both as a professional and as a company. With the right approach and leadership, crisis recovery can be a positive time for an organization, a period of renewal and a recommitment to the core principles under which the organization was founded. It may not seem like it at the time, when you're handling slings and arrows from every direction, but you *can* come out a stronger individual and company.

✦ Words of Wisdom from Fairy Godparents ✦

"The question isn't who is going to let me; it's who is going to stop me."

—Ayn Rand, novelist and philosopher

Here are some of our prescriptions for making a full recovery from a crisis that leaves you better off than you were before.

Tips for Turning a Royal Pain Into a Positive

★ **Find the positive.** Sometimes life deals you a bad card without warning, and there is no way you could have foreseen or prevented it. It's important not to dwell on the negative, but rather try to see the positive in any given scenario. For example, if you are receiving some negative feedback on your product, recognize that this is an opportunity to learn more about how you can improve your offering. Engage in a productive dialogue with the people who are complaining, and turn a detractor into a new brand evangelist.

★ **Learn a lesson.** You can always learn from bad situations, even though you may not have been able to prevent them. Take note of how you handled yourself in the situation by writing down what you did well and what you could have worked on. Turn it into a learning experience and make a new plan to follow in the future if necessary.

★ **Determine a worst-case scenario.** Asking yourself "What's the worst that can happen?"—closely followed by "Does it matter? Does it *really* matter?"—can often really help in unexpected situations. You will probably find that the worst-case scenario is not likely to happen—and even if it does, if you stay calm and respond strategically, you can recover. And remember, whatever doesn't kill you makes you stronger!

★ **Get some perspective.** Examine the situation and determine what caused the disaster strike. Take a step back and find a different perspective. What's happened to you probably could have been a lot worse and isn't a big deal in the larger scheme of things.

★ **Be decisive.** Make decisions and act. You may not always make the very best decision, but you will be doing something, and it is that something that really matters.

★ **Get a healthy outside opinion.** If you are unable to get rid of negative thoughts surrounding an event, seek out someone you trust and feel comfortable speaking with. Often talking about what went wrong with someone not involved in the situation really helps, and allows you to reevaluate what happened in a positive way. He or she will most likely be able to reassure you that what happened wasn't as detrimental as you think.

★ **Switch gears.** If you're really feeling down on yourself and can't shake off negative thoughts, throw yourself into a hobby or community cause to take your mind off things and see the world in a positive light.

★ **Try to move on.** Life doesn't always go your way, and there will be many times when you have to do things you don't want to do. You could complain and choose to see only the negative, or you could choose to be the bigger person and just roll with it. You never know—it may just be the best thing that could have happened.

★ **Look forward.** Since you can't change the past, accept what has happened and look forward to the future.

★ **Don't fear change.** Change is not always a negative. Often it is a positive. But whether the change is good or not, it is a part of life and is often something that we cannot control. The best way to cope with unwanted change is to accept it and adjust your plans accordingly.

Cinderella CEO Q&A

Therese McPherson
Freelancer extraordinaire
www.theresemcpherson.com

Tell us a little bit about your background.

I am Therese McPherson, and there is nothing I want more than to pay back my student loans ($150,000) and give my children more than I had. I don't come from much. My adoptive parents came from poverty. My father was a truck driver and my mother is disabled with a heart and lung disease. I watched my father rise up from being at the bottom of his company to becoming the branch manager and taking over three stores across his state.

I was a very curious and rough kid. My father later told me that it was his goal to make sure that I never had to depend on anyone and that I could always find my way up from the bottom, no matter how low I got.

At the age of six, I was walking around my block knocking on doors, asking if I could wash my neighbors' cars. By the age of ten, I ran my first lawn service company. I taught myself to run piping underground and install fountains, I weeded, tended to rose bushes, then started fixing my customers' broken stereos. I bought my first Apple laptop from that job. I wanted the laptop so I could record myself making music. I taught myself Garage Band software and started to make multitrack recordings. I also taught myself to read music, draw, paint, speak some

Russian, Spanish, and Italian, play the bass, drums, guitar, build half pipes, tree forts, and sew. I played a lot, learned a lot. I wanted to be a scientist, a singer, a doctor, a lawyer, a chef, a TV personality, a musician, an engineer, an athlete, a professional skateboarder, a painter, a teacher, a photojournalist, a writer. I wanted to do everything. I still do. It's hard to settle. I eventually learned I could do whatever I wanted. I have an entire lifetime to do a lot of things.

I am a generalist. A jack of all trades, a master of none. I am infinitely interested. I know a little bit about a lot. When I went to college, I went for fine art, so I could study anything I wanted and work it conceptually into a studio practice. While in college, my first year, my dad hit his mid-life crisis and spent all the money he had saved for college . . . and his retirement. He left my mother and grandmother in complete poverty and dropped me completely. I had no money at all. I slept on floors and fit my whole life in my car. Eventually, I saved a little money and rented a house with some friends. We lived in a ghetto where we had to screw our windows shut. Our neighbors would get robbed at gunpoint and we would drop to the floor. Every night there were gunshots. It wasn't a safe place at all. I struggled hard to get out of there.

⋆⁺⋆ Words of Wisdom from Fairy Godparents ⋆⁺⋆

"I learned to always take on things I'd never done before. Growth and comfort do not coexist."

—Virginia Rometty, CEO of IBM

I started making little movies with the laptop my school gave me upon admission. They eventually got noticed and I was hired to film guest speakers that came into the Fine Art Department. I had no clue what I was doing, but I researched online and tried hard to learn on my own. My motto was, "Fake it till you make it" and I did.

I took on video clients and completely failed on their projects, but I learned from my mistakes and continued to try. I also started teaching pre-K kids. I also worked as a muralist. I worked two to three jobs at all times while in college. By my senior year, I was the first fine art student to be hired full-time by the college's Design Center. I made all of their marketing videos. When I graduated I sold them a marketing package that moved me to New York, where I opened my first business. I also started teaching art lessons to elementary, middle school, and high school students in the Hudson Valley. I ran a green screen studio upstate and searched for work in the city. I landed a good gig and moved myself here.

I have been working freelance full-time since I graduated college three years ago. I have made music videos featured on *Billboard* and sponsored by Pepsi, pieces featured in the MoMa, on Nickmom.com, *Harpers Bazaar*'s website, in-store displays at Macys, *Elle*, Complex Media, private art collections, and museums. I have explored preproduction, production, and postproduction. I do a lot of things. I am not afraid to try something new and expand my skill set.

Do you have any words of wisdom for other young entrepreneurs?

Collaborate sooner. Burn no bridges. Believe in others—they will grow too; they will do good things. Leave every place you go better than when you arrived. Have standards and know yourself well, well enough that you are confident and comfortable in your own skin. Integrity: value it. Avoid romanticizing, be real. Take care of your body and mind. Never leave a job until you have another one. Don't let your bank account get low, work three jobs if you have to, you should always be able to lose your job and live for a year off of your savings. Never think that you are too good to take out the trash, and never think you aren't good enough to make something big happen. Fail as hard as you possibly can and take on the biggest challenges, because then you will grow. Remember to always grow, and to be as current as possible. All you have to do is do what you want to do, the fear of failure can be stifling, so don't allow yourself to procrastinate. Start today.

Do you have a guilty pleasure?

I have no guilt in my pleasure, but I love skateboarding, when I have time I take my board and put my headphones on and hit it.

What's the best tip you've ever received on success?

Success is an idea, it's nothing you can grasp, and it's something different to everyone. So I would say figure out what success is to you. Above all, make yourself happy and manage your stress. I think if you are a happy go-getter who isn't afraid to fail, then you will learn to succeed at whatever you desire.

Chapter 8's Cinderella Principles

Be prepared: Increase your ability to quickly recover from a bad situation by defining crises, assigning responsibilities, and communicating with your staff and your customers.

Respond properly: Don't panic! Use actions and words in an organized way to show others you care.

Make a full recovery: Turn the negative into a positive by examining the situation and evaluating your response, and take away valuable lessons for next time.

CHAPTER 9

If the Glass Slipper Fits, Wear It

★

ENJOY YOUR SUCCESS

$\mathcal{A}$ few days later, the king's son had it proclaimed, by sound of trumpet, that he would marry her whose foot this slipper would just fit. They began to try it on the princesses, then the duchesses and all the court, but in vain; it was brought to the two sisters, who did all they possibly could to force their foot into the slipper, but they did not succeed.

Cinderella, who saw all this, and knew that it was her slipper, said to them, laughing, "Let me see if it will not fit me."

Her sisters burst out laughing, and began to banter with her. The gentleman who was sent to try the slipper looked earnestly at Cinderella, and, finding her very handsome, said that it was only just that she should try as well, and that he had orders to let everyone try.

He had Cinderella sit down, and, putting the slipper to her foot, he found that it went on very easily, fitting her as if it had been made of wax. Her two sisters were greatly astonished, but then even more so, when Cinderella pulled out of her pocket the other slipper, and put it on her other foot. Then in came her godmother and touched her wand to Cinderella's clothes, making them richer and more magnificent than any of those she had worn before.

Take What's Yours

When opportunity finally knocks on Cinderella's door, it's her wicked stepsisters who first step up to claim the prize that is rightfully hers. And even when Cinderella herself steps up and asks to try on her glass slipper, everybody laughs at her. They can't believe her nerve! But Cinderella knows that it's now or never. This is her moment, she earned it, and she seizes opportunity and success when they finally knock on her door. It is only because Cinderella is able to stand up and accept success that her dreams actually come true.

For many Cinderella CEOs, failure can be a lot less scary than success, and when we finally do manage to make our dreams come true, we can feel more stressed out than happy. We slam the door on destiny when it finally arrives, and send our big opportunity packing. But as all reigning Cinderella CEOs will tell you, when your moment comes, you have to seize it, because it may not come again.

⋆٭⋆ Words of Wisdom from Fairy Godparents ٭⋆٭

"The only way to do something in depth is to work hard. The moment you start being in love with what you're doing, and thinking it's beautiful or rich, then you're in danger."

—Miuccia Prada, fashion designer and owner of Prada

Owning your value and talent, having the confidence to ask for what you're entitled to, charging what you're worth, and managing the royal treasure responsibly are all tools that you will need in order to claim your success. Feeling deserving of success is the very first building block in a strong professional and personal foundation that will allow you and your business to live happily ever after.

ROYAL ROLE MODEL

Shree Bose
Student, Cancer Researcher
www.shreebose.com

> *"The feeling of accomplishment when you actually have*
> *gone through the entire process of finding your own problem*
> *and getting a hypothesis, and doing your tests and getting*
> *your results is just the most amazing feeling."*

—Shree Bose

When Shree's beloved grandfather was dying of liver cancer, Shree wanted to do something about it. She wanted to fight cancer, and help others survive. As a fifteen-year-old high school student, however, her scientific research opportunities were limited. She reached out to various hospitals and research facilities, trying to find a way to get involved with cancer research, but no one took her seriously. After all, she was just a teenager with no medical experience whatsoever. She received dozens of rejections, but Shree didn't let that stop her. Finally, she heard from the North Texas Science Health Center, who had no such reservations. Instead, they chose to mentor her, and that is how Shree became involved with cancer research at only fifteen years old.

Bose chose to study the protein AMP kinase and its reaction with the chemotherapy drug cisplatin. She noticed that when she inhibited this protein, cisplatin was allowed to begin destroying cancer cells once again. Shree's response to her family's health crisis and the work it inspired has provided a newer, more effective, treatment regime for the more than 240,000 patients diagnosed with ovarian cancer each year who have developed resistance to available drugs. As a result of her accomplishments, at only eighteen years old, Shree won the Grand Prize at the first-ever Google global science fair. Shree is currently studying molecular biology at Harvard and plans to go to medical school. Eventually, she would like to be a physician and a medical researcher.

What Type of Company Are You Running?

We know, this part can be a bit daunting—but you can't rule over a golden age of your business if you don't know how to manage legal documents and the royal treasury. The first thing you will have to decide is what kind of a business organization you want to become. Think this through carefully, and speak to an accountant or tax professional, because this decision will not only impact how much you pay in taxes, but will affect all that you do. The most common forms of business for young entrepreneurs are sole proprietorships, corporations, or partnerships.

If you decide to start your business as a sole proprietorship but later decide to take on partners, you can reorganize with partners. Following is more information about each option.

Sole Proprietorship

Selecting the sole proprietorship business structure means you are personally responsible for your company's liabilities. As a result, you are placing your assets at risk and they could be seized to satisfy a business debt, so be careful in your spending and budgeting. Most small businesses that are service-driven—such as writers, artists, musicians, craftspeople, or consultants of any kind—start out with this model. It is the simplest from a legal perspective, and allows you to grow to a size where becoming a corporation starts to make more sense.

Corporation

The corporate structure is more complex and expensive than most other business structures. A corporation is an independent legal entity, separate from its owners, and as such, it requires complying with more regulations and tax requirements. The biggest benefit for a business owner who decides to incorporate is the liability protection he or she receives. Once you have grown past the point where you are just one person in your bedroom providing goods and services for a price, and begin to hire staff and generate significant revenue, it is time to think about reorganizing as a corporation, which would provide greater protection of your personal assets.

Partnership

If your business will be owned and operated by several individuals, you'll want to take a look at structuring your business as a partnership. Partnerships come in two varieties: general partnerships and limited partnerships. Unless you expect to have many passive investors, limited partnerships are generally not the best choice for a new business because of all the required filings and administrative matters.

The Art of Negotiating

One key skill you'll have to learn as you run your business is how to negotiate effectively. In fact, most people negotiate in some way almost every day. If you are going to be in business for yourself—or even conduct everyday business of any kind, from buying a car to planning a birthday party—you are going to have to learn how to negotiate effectively, responsibly, and productively. The best negotiation is one in which everybody walks away from the table satisfied and ready to live up to their part of the bargain. If this situation is not a win-win, then generally you run into trouble down the line. If you make a killing but leave your client or customer feeling overly pressured, then that client will be much harder to please when it comes to delivery. If you shortchange yourself, you will not only impede your own business growth but also probably wind up feeling resentful to boot. When you are feeling undervalued or taken advantage of, you seldom deliver your best work.

Fortunately, there are some very useful guidelines for how to conduct a positive and productive negotiation and come out with a win-win that leaves everybody feeling good about the relationship. But negotiating, like anything in life, takes practice. The more you practice and perfect the following skills, the better you will get at driving a hard, but fair, bargain

Know What You're Worth

Rule number one in any negotiation is to know what you're worth. The second is to feel entitled to ask for a fair price for your services. Calculate what your costs are, consider the time involved, consider your level of talent, and charge accordingly.

If you are unsure what a fair price is for your level of expertise, check out the competition. Do your research. Figure out how much to charge for goods and services by taking a look at what similar products and services are going for in your area. What is different about your product or service? Does that make it worth more or less? Knowing the market will be imperative to calculating your worth and driving a fair deal in exchange for your goods and services. Most important, however, is that you appreciate and value what you have to offer, or you will never get anybody else to feel the same way.

Slow and Steady Wins the Race

People drive the worst bargains when they are under pressure or in a hurry. That's a relatively easy problem to solve: Never feel rushed in a negotiation. Leave yourself plenty of time and be prepared to wait out a negotiation. The person who has time on her side is always in a more powerful position at the bargaining table. Be patient, be firm, and be in a position to wait for the other party to come around to your way of thinking.

Make a Mean Face

This sounds ridiculous. We get that, but . . .

The mean face is one of the oldest and most effective negotiation tactics! A mean face is a visible reaction to an offer or price. The objective of this negotiation tactic is to make the other people feel uncomfortable about the offer they presented. And this works when you are on either side of the negotiating table. Sometimes the "mean" face is actually one of shock or surprise.

For example, when we were looking for an office space, we asked the real estate agent, "You want how much?!" The key is to appear completely shocked that they could be bold enough to name that number. People will respond in one of three ways:

1. They will become very uncomfortable and begin to try to rationalize their price.
2. They will offer an immediate concession.
3. They won't change the price and you have to decide what your move will be.

In our case, we were offered an immediate concession. It wasn't a lot less money but low enough that we could afford the office space. Practice this move in a mirror or with a friend so you feel comfortable using it when the time comes.

Do Your Homework

This is a particularly important negotiation tactic. Information is power, and the more you know about what you are selling or buying and who you are selling to or buying from, the better armed you will be in a negotiation. Ask questions. Learn what is important to them as well as what their needs and desires are. Develop the habit of asking yourself these questions before you make a big investment or purchase:

★ Why should I purchase now?
★ Have I done enough research?
★ What timing am I looking at?
★ Why is this important to me?

It is also important to learn as much about your competitors as possible. This will help you defeat possible price objections and prevent someone from using your competitor as leverage. If, for example, you are looking to rent an office space, find out how much comparable offices cost in the neighborhood. Investigate how much the units are going for in the building you are interested in, and what the rents were in the past. Research the plans for the neighborhood and assess the future growth of the area and how much rates might rise, making it a good or a bad idea to lock in at a rate right now. If you wait, conditions could improve or could get worse. In any negotiation, information is power, so gather as much of it as you possibly can. It will increase your leverage at the bargaining table.

Use Your Negotiating Wand at Every Opportunity

Most people hesitate to negotiate because they lack the confidence. Asking for money in exchange for your services, or asking for a discount on something you want to acquire that you feel is overpriced, requires self-assurance and self-confidence. Develop this confidence by negotiating more frequently. Remember to be pleasant and persistent but not overbearing. Try out a few of the following incantations and see what kind of a deal you can conjure up.

Say the Magic Words

* ★ You can do better than that.
* ★ We are a startup without a lot of capital; do you offer any kind of a discount for entrepreneurs?
* ★ That's too expensive. Can you do any better than that?
* ★ I'm sorry, that number isn't possible for me. Is there any way we can figure out a situation that works for us both?
* ★ Would you consider a barter arrangement?

Remember, You Might Need to Walk Away

Enter every negotiation with the understanding that you can and will walk away from the bargaining table if necessary. If you need a deal too badly, and feel that you must make something work no matter what, then you seriously undermine your leverage. If you won't walk away, there is no reason for anyone to meet your terms. It is better to walk away from a sale rather than make too large a concession or give a deep discount on your product or service.

CINDERELLA CEO PROFILE

Heidi Dangelmaier
Girlapproved
www.girlapproved.us

> *"I used the experience of feeling like an outsider to create new things that make other people feel more included."*
>
> —Heidi Dangelmaier

Heidi is a scientist, inventor, and designer who earned her doctorate in computer science and physics at Princeton. She pioneered early video games for girls at Sega and Electronic Arts, and she founded the first female web tech firm, Hi-D. A trailblazer in social media, Hi-D invented and sold social apps to megabrands like CBS, Comedy Central, Coca-Cola, and Samsung, years before Facebook was even a twinkle in Mark Zuckerberg's eye. Heidi doesn't only fit in in a computer lab full of nerds—she is a Renaissance woman with street cred in pop culture, design, and marketing. She is not just a theorist; she is a hands-on creative, building mass-market products, brands, fashion, and tech.

For nearly a decade, Heidi has run Girlapproved (*www.girlapproved .us*), the first all-girl innovation firm. Girlapproved mobilizes young female talent to compete against the world's largest research, strategy, and design firms in the nation. GA spent a quarter of their time working with corporate clients, and the rest operating a research lab/think tank. During this eight-year period, Heidi and the girls have helped create and launch new brands, products, fashion, entertainment, pop culture, and apps, as well as turned around old ones from many major brands including Unilever, Nokia, P&G, Jones, J&J, Merck, Abercrombie, Crayola, and Rubbermaid.

Open with the Best Terms You Can Logically Argue For

The moment you set a price, what you are actually doing is establishing a ballpark for your services. Once you mention a price for your services with a buyer, the only place you have to go is down, so start as high as you can. It makes you look like you are giving more ground than you actually are when you back off your original sticker price.

If you are the buyer, open with the lowest amount you could possibly offer without being insulting, at which point you run the risk of them exercising their power to walk away and souring the whole deal!

Shop Around

Whether you are buying or selling, the more you have shopped around, the more you will know about what constitutes a good deal. If you have found a better deal elsewhere, bring proof. If you know that you are reasonably priced within your industry, say so. Be ready to back up your offers with cold, hard facts by shopping around and learning the realities of your marketplace.

Don't Say the First Thing That Pops Into Your Head

When someone proposes terms, or argues with your own, wait a moment before responding. You don't have to say the first thing that pops into your head. Use the silence—let their words hang in the air a moment, think about your response, and let the silence tell them you are dissatisfied.

✦ Words of Wisdom from Fairy Godparents ✦

"We cannot change what we are not aware of, and once we are aware, we cannot help but change."

—Sheryl Sandberg, COO of Facebook

Be Prepared to Make Some Concessions

You have to give in order to get. If you are expecting someone you are negotiating with to give up something that they want, you are going to have to meet them halfway. On the other hand, never give away anything or make a concession without getting something in return. Try to find ways to sweeten the deal that aren't that painful for you, but if you will not budge from your original position, you will not be in a negotiation—you will be out the door. Ask for something that's valuable to you but doesn't cost them very much, or conversely, offer something that is valuable to them but not that difficult for you. For example, you may be able to move quickly if they have a pressing deadline, or wait longer to start a deal. Flexibility in your own schedule can be worth better terms if the person you are negotiating with is more tied to a schedule than you.

Always Hold Back a Closer

Don't offer everything upfront. Gradually negotiate a deal, withholding a few key concessions or incentives that you are willing to throw in at the end if you absolutely have to in order to make a deal go through. Offer this too early and you may have given away something that you didn't need to, or wind up having to bend further than you're willing to in order to close.

Don't Let Personal Hang-ups Sidetrack the Negotiations

Negotiating a deal is business, and demands a professional demeanor and a professional perspective if you are going to be successful. Don't let personal issues enter the conversation or the situation. For example, wanting something too badly can make you offer concessions that are not in your best interests. Envision what you want out of the situation, what is fair, and go after that.

Royal Role Model Q&A

Sayako Quinlan

What are your goals and aspirations?

Hello! My name is Sayako Quinlan and I will be heading to Georgetown University School of Foreign Service in 2015. I am going into the school undeclared, but after a recent trip to D.C. for the university's open house, I am leaning toward a major in Culture and Politics. My dream is to become a Foreign Service Officer (the United States' version of a diplomat) or in some other way work for the State Department.

Do you have any words of wisdom to share with other young women?

This is a tough question for me to answer because, as a seventeen-year-old, I have yet to experience many things in life and one needs experience to be able to give wisdom. So, I will speak from what I have experienced. Be an open-minded individual. Open-mindedness allows us to be constantly learning especially from those who we might completely disagree with. Even so, we should listen to those opinions and those stories because they could either open up a new perspective for us or reaffirm our belief in our previous stance. That is where the "individual" part comes in. Listen, understand, and then decide for ourselves what we believe and what we want.

How has ballet helped define you as a person?

My favorite part of ballet is class. I do love performing, but I would choose class over a performance every day. Ballet class empowers me with discipline and control over myself that carries over into my daily life. At the same time, it is during class that I can try new technique, strive for new skills, and experiment with new artistry. I appreciate routine and I embrace pandemonium.

How do you stay focused?

I do what I want and I want what I do. This may sound crazy, but I do want to do homework. I want to do homework because it helps me learn new things, gives me a sense of accomplishment, and means that I will have free time after. I want to stay thirty minutes after ballet class to rehearse my solo because it makes me better at what I love to do (and I am getting more exercise!). I want to spend two hours of my Sunday morning knocking on doors for a congressional campaign because I want to inform voters and I want to enjoy the lovely weather. Focus comes from motivation.

Tips for Running the Royal Budget

Managing your finances and measuring your growth are building blocks of a company's success. But before you can expect to manage the financial health of your realm, you will need to create a budget.

Budgets need to be realistic, never fabricated. Numbers do not lie. Ever. By being on top of your budget, you might be able to make changes with expenses before it's too late. There are basically two types of budgets:

1. **Capital expenditure** (also known as "CapEx") captures costs associated with equipment. This is equipment that generally lasts for more than a year, such as a computer.
2. **Operating budget,** which is related to the normal day-to-day operations and expenditures such as payroll, supplies, and miscellaneous.

The key to financial success, particularly in the very beginning of your business when income is small, is to set a budget and stick to it. If you go over it, you have to make sure you have a credit line or savings to cover the spending you made over your projected budget.

Starting a Budget

While you have already projected a budget in your business plan, once you are actually in the throes of your business, you will need to track the realities of having a new business. The best way to begin a reality-based budget is to keep track of all expenses and income for one month. After the first month, take stock of what you've spent and what you've earned, and compile your actual budget. In addition to controlling expenses, tracking earnings and expenses can give you a lot of valuable information about how to grow and expand your business without winding up in royal debt.

Following is a list that will help you collect all the financial information you need to make a budget:

★ Decide what time frame you will be reviewing your business (quarterly, monthly, yearly).
★ Project your expenses and record the sales you need to achieve in order to meet those obligations.
★ Gather sales reports/invoices and record all money brought in. (Tip: We like Quicken as a great software that helps you organize all of this.)

Once you have a list of all your income and expenses, you can take the dollar amount brought in and subtract from it the money you spent. The result is your profit (or loss).

Once you have an idea of the size of your profit or loss, and what your expenses are over a six- to twelve-month period, you can create a financial forecast so you will never be off guard, and can set realistic goals for growth.

·· Words of Wisdom from Fairy Godparents ·*·*

"Our deepest fear is not that we are inadequate. Our deepest fear is that we are powerful beyond measure. It is our light, not our darkness that most frightens us. We ask ourselves, 'Who am I to be brilliant, gorgeous, talented, fabulous?' Actually, who are you not to be? You are a child of God. Your playing small does not serve the world. There is nothing enlightened about shrinking so that other people won't feel insecure around you. We are all meant to shine."

—Marianne Williamson, author

Financial Glossary

Here are a few other terms you should be familiar with when it comes to interpreting financial growth and planning accordingly.

★ Accounts Receivable—money that other people owe you. You don't actually have this money to spend until they pay you, so set up payment collection systems in order to get your cash in a timely manner. There are multiple ways to do that, such as setting up a direct deposit through your bank. Another option is a website like Shopify (*www.shopify.com*), which allows you to set up online accounts.

* Accounts Payable—money that you owe your vendors.
* Costs—the amount of money you spend providing services and on your business each period, such as the cost of producing the things you sell, monthly subscription services, hosting fees, salaries, rent, office costs.
* Forecasting—planning a budget ahead of time. Compare your previous budgets with your actual spending and earnings; this will help you set goals for the future.
* Profit—what's left after you subtract your expenses from your income.
* Revenue—the amount of money you generate from sales each period.

Spend Your Money Wisely

Beyond tracking your expenses and keeping your eye on the royal till, how you manage your money in general will make the difference between a successful venture and a not-so-successful one. Learn good spending habits, be resourceful wherever you can, and avoid the pitfalls that can sink the realm right before your eyes. Here are some ideas to help you spend like a sound and reliable queen of your kingdom.

* When you can, borrow or rent, don't buy.
* If you have the money, pay a high down payment, meaning pay more of the loan upfront—this will benefit you in the long run and you will thank yourself when you pay less interest on the loan overall.
* Understand that owning a credit card and charging things to it each month and paying it off on time will be very important for establishing credit.
* Spend what you have, not what you hope to make.

Make Smart Investments

You might eventually find yourself in a place where you have enough profits that you want to invest them in other ways. Then your profits will be earning money for you while you figure out how to use them for your business. Consider getting the advice of a professional in this case—there are a lot of options and you want to be well educated before you dive in.

Build Your Savings

Whether you decide to invest or not, you should always have an eye on building a nice cushion of savings in your business. This rainy-day fund will help you in many ways down the road.

★ Start by saving as much of your expendable income as possible.
★ Start an emergency fund that contains three to six months' worth of expenses. This way, you can be sure that your business has the liquidity to survive the ups and downs that any new entrepreneurial adventure will have to weather.

Cinderella CEO Q&A

Michaela d'Artois
www.instagram.com/michaeladartois

Tell us a little about your background.

My name is Michaela d'Artois and I am a journalist living in San Francisco, CA. My career in fashion was pretty much set from a young age, stemming from a strong need to express myself through the sartorial starting at four. When I realized my love for writing, and the energy I gained from meeting like-minded people—my path kind of decided itself. I got my degree from The Academy of Art University in fashion journalism, and have since had the pleasure of working with some amazing publications.

Do you have any words of wisdom for other young entrepreneurs?

I believe that it is in you to succeed for yourself and no one else. At the end of the day, who you dress for, whom you work hard for, and whom you love most should always be you. If you are too busy waiting for your Prince Charming to hand-deliver your glass slipper, you are going to miss out on a lot of things, including buying yourself Prada slippers, and that is a feeling I suggest not missing out on. Your positive energy will fling doors open.

Who are your fashion icons?

My icons are the women who are brave enough to dress in a way that forces people to ask questions, and who aren't afraid to show their powerful side—because that's sexy. These are ladies such as Catherine Baba and Simone de Beauvoir. But above ALL, cue my fashion soulmate, Carine Roitfeld.

How do you stay focused as a writer?

I think seeing the end goal—seeing my writing in print fuels that flame. It's not that I don't get distracted, but writing being my number one love, I always come back to the notebook/keyboard. I also believe that creating tangible works is a great addition to giving back.

How has writing helped define you as a person?

Writing has helped define me in my personal work, as it's my way of untangling my ideas, surroundings, and life in general. Once I have it all on paper, it's much easier for me to figure things out. In my work it has helped me find a voice in the fashion industry, which I can cultivate throughout my career, and knowing that knowledge lays ahead is a great thing. The more I work, the more I learn and the better my writing gets, at least that's what I hope is happening!

How do you stay on top of trends?

I try not to engage in too many; I think that's the key. I love knowing the zeitgeist of the current culture, but picking trends that are only true to you will keep you from any serious style blunders.

Chapter 9's Cinderella Principles

Embrace negotiating: It's a way of life. Most people negotiate in some way almost every day.

Know what you're worth: Rule number one in any negotiation is to know what you're worth.

Manage your money like a queen: Beyond tracking your expenses and keeping your eye on the royal till, how you manage your money in general will make the difference between a successful venture and a not so successful one.

Know that establishing a good company culture doesn't mean you have to be cheap: Find ways to maintain good company morale and balance profits with money you put back into the company.

Choose the correct business setup for your company: Look into your options and talk to a professional about setting up the correct legal entity.

Rule over a Golden Age

And now her two sisters found her to be that fine, beautiful lady whom they had seen at the ball. They threw themselves at her feet to beg pardon for all the ill treatment they had made her undergo. Cinderella took them up, and, as she embraced them, said that she forgave them with all her heart, and wanted them always to love her.

She was taken to the young prince, dressed as she was. He thought she was more charming than before, and, a few days after, married her. Cinderella, who was no less good than beautiful, gave her two sisters lodgings in the palace, and that very same day matched them with two great lords of the court.

Once Cinderella becomes a princess, the fate of her wicked stepmother and evil stepsisters is left up to her. Yet, despite all of their cruelty to her over the years, Cinderella does not use her power to punish her wicked stepsisters. Instead, she uses her power to forgive them and include them in her success, because Cinderella understands that the only happy reign is a peaceful reign, where everybody lives in balance and harmony.

Even princesses have to obey the golden rule, and live their lives and run their businesses with the same kindness, understanding, fairness, and forgiveness that Cinderella demonstrates at the end of her tale. And that doesn't only apply to other people. You also have to be a kind and beneficent ruler over yourself. Often, and especially when you are embarking on a new business, it's easy to forget to set some time aside for the other important areas of your life.

Your relationships with your family and your friends—and more importantly, your relationship with yourself and the things that you enjoy—can begin to take a back seat to the business. When this happens, you can begin to lose your balance, and before you know it you are toppling from the throne. So remember that all work and no play is more than just dull—it's unhealthy, and can't be sustained over the long haul without serious consequences to your kingdom.

A big part of making sure that your dreams of happily ever after really do come true is keeping your dream from turning into a nightmare because you lose track of yourself and what makes you happy, or are doggedly pursuing a dream that just isn't working out the way you thought it would. You have to stay agile, inspired, healthy, and connected to the people, places, and things that brought you here in the first place.

The Happily Ever After First Year Self-Assessment Tool

It's important as a part of your overall business growth strategy to set aside some time on a regular basis—once a month, once a quarter, or twice a year—to take stock and assess what is working and what isn't from a holistic point of view. Success is about more than money; it's about a lot of intangibles that can get lost in the budget.

The Happily Ever After quiz that you filled out at the beginning of this book is a great tool to use when you are ready to make your first regular assessment of how your dream launch is going. Take a look at the answers that you wrote down at the beginning of your new company, and ask yourself the new set of the following questions about your reactions to what you wrote way back when, before you really knew what you were in for!

Question #1: Are you happy with the people in your personal and professional life?

A big part of happily ever after is being surrounded by people, both professionally and personally, who respect, inspire, support, and engage you. Successful people surround themselves with people who make them better.

- ★ What kind of people have you attracted into your royal entourage in your first year of business? Are they the people that you set out to attract? Are they different?
- ★ Have people been nicer and more helpful than you expected? Or more difficult than you expected?
- ★ How have your personal relationships changed in the course of the last year, if at all? Have you made new friends? Have you kept the old?
- ★ Thinking ahead to the next year of your business, what would you change about the people that currently surround and support you, and what would you keep the same?

_____

_____

_____

_____

_____

Question #2: Are you happy with your surroundings?

How you feel about your immediate surroundings, and the environment that shapes your life, is a central component in long-term business and personal health.

★ What kinds of places did you think your business would take you to in the beginning? Has it taken you to any of them?

★ Has your business led you to discover new and exciting places that exceeded expectations?

★ Have you been disappointed in any way with the places your business has taken you to?

★ Do you spend enough time in places that you love, or not enough?

★ What would you change about your physical world in the coming year if you could?

★ What can you absolutely not do without for your company? This can be anything from an actual office space to a fancy coffee machine.

_____

_____

_____

_____

_____

Question #3: Do you like what you do?

What did you imagine yourself doing every day when you first embarked on your business? It's time to look at your day-to-day life.

★ In the last year, did you actually wind up doing what you envisioned or are your activities and tasks different than you anticipated?

★ Are you happy in your current lifestyle?

★ Do you like the actual work involved in building your business?

★ Which parts do you like best? Which tasks would you rather do away with or delegate?

★ What parts of your business are you best at?

★ Have you learned to do new things that you never knew you could do or enjoy before?

★ Have you found that there are things you thought you would enjoy, but you don't?

★ In the coming year, what would you like to do more of, and what would you like to do less of?

_____

_____

_____

_____

_____

Question #4: Are you happy with your business culture?

Think back to the kind of culture you were looking for when you began this process.

★ Have you created a culture in your business that expresses what you feel strongly about?

★ Have you created a lifestyle for yourself in tandem with your brand that meets your needs personally, as well as professionally?

★ Do the people who work for and with you feel good about their experience at your business?

★ What are the pillars of your business culture as it exists today?

★ How would you like to see your business culture change or be sustained in the next year?

_____

_____

_____

_____

_____

Question #5: Are you serving causes that you are passionate about?

Think back about what you wanted to stand for when you started your business. What ideals, values, and causes were you willing to fight for or against?

- ★ Have you remained passionate about the same things over the last year, or have your views changed?
- ★ Is your business making the kind of contribution to the world that you had anticipated?
- ★ Are you profiting with purpose?
- ★ Do you feel fulfilled spiritually by your work?
- ★ If you could commit to a new set of objectives for the coming year, what would those be? Or would they stay the same?

_____

_____

_____

_____

_____

Cinderella's Tips for Maintaining a Work-Life Balance

While we will never know what became of Cinderella once she rode off into the sunset with her handsome prince, it's a pretty safe bet that at some point she was going to have to learn how to take off the gown and the crown, and kick up her heels and relax and enjoy her success and her royal marriage. Here are some tips that we have gathered over the years to make sure that you manage your work-life balance like a queen.

* **Prioritize and delegate:** When you are used to being in charge of everything, it can be hard to avoid feeling that you have to do everything by yourself, and quickly. Learn to set priorities. Don't try to do everything at once. And don't be afraid to delegate. You can't run a kingdom by yourself without compromising quality, so learn how to engage the help of your staff to get things done, and in the right order of priority.

* **Have realistic expectations of yourself and others:** Nobody can be the best at everything all the time. Mistakes will happen, opportunities get missed, and occasionally, you lose a battle or two. Set reasonable and reachable goals, don't insist on a perfect record, and keep in mind that you are all human, and that sometimes the greatest discoveries arise out of what once looked like a mistake or a failure.

* **Set goals that are just a little out of your reach, but not too high to achieve, and revisit them often:** It's important to set the bar high, and reimagine your personal best with each new year in business. Setting goals that are unattainable, however, can quickly frustrate you and your staff and take all the wind out of your sails. That kind of drop in morale only impedes growth and erodes your team's sense of accomplishment and self-esteem. And this ultimately impacts performance and growth. Take time with yourself, and with your team, to assess your progress and your goals to make sure that everyone is on the same page and feeling productive and satisfied with the progress.

* **Business is personal:** It's important to realize that people, even professional people, have feelings, and that includes you. Don't lose touch with how you and the people in your life are feeling about things. If you are feeling overwhelmed, stressed, angry, or underserved, you should acknowledge your feel-

ings and express them directly to those involved. Bottling things up, ignoring or denying your true feelings, and carrying on anyway makes it impossible for you and the other people involved to identify problems and solve them before they get out of hand and do damage to your business culture.

★ **Don't forget your health:** In order to access the kind of clarity and energy that is required to build a successful business, you have to remember to take care of your body as well as your brand. Get enough sleep, eat right, take time to exercise, meditate—and above all, discover ways to relax and release the stress that you will inevitably encounter as a growing new brand.

★ **Have fun:** All work and no play is not a good rule for any realm. You have to stay engaged with the people, places, and things that bring you pleasure separate and apart from your business. Continuing to grow as a business means continuing to grow as a person, and you can't do that unless you are living life to the fullest and having some good old-fashioned fun.

Happiness Is a Journey

As you probably have realized after comparing where you are now with where you thought you would be when you filled out your Happily Ever After quiz, "happily ever after" is a fluid concept. It changes as you learn and grow, and you have to be flexible enough to keep up with the pace of what your development is demanding of you.

Some things that we think are going to make us happy don't turn out to be so terrific once they have become a reality. And some things that we never imagined ourselves doing turn out to be second nature, and some of our very favorite things. This is part of the wonderful and ever-unfolding mystery of growth in life and growth in a business, so it's important to take stock and adjust your course if you want to continue to rule over a truly golden age.

Hold on to your answers to these questions, and use them as a basis of comparison each year to assess where you are and where you want to be. This tool will keep you in touch with where you came from, and help you get where you are going armed with the understanding of where you have been. Like Cinderella, you want to acknowledge your past—but always be looking ahead to your future in the palace.

Resources

Websites

Blinksale

www.blinksale.com

This site has online options for invoicing.

Brazen Careerist

www.brazencareerist.com

Career advice from recruiters.

Education.com

www.education.com

Read articles on young entrepreneurs and tips on successful teens for inspiration.

Girls Inc.

www.girlsinc.org

Promotes a girl's right to be herself!

Heart of Gold Girls

www.heartofgoldgirls.com

Provides an online environment that shares tools, information, and inspiration to connect with your passion.

LinkedIn

www.LinkedIn.com

This professional network allows you to connect and reach out to potential employers, show off your resume, and gain information on various careers or career you are pursuing.

Market Like a Chick

www.twitter.com/MarketLikeAChik

Forbes Top 30 Women Entrepreneur on Twitter, marketing advice.

Mind Tools

www.mindtools.com

This site provides tips and tools on how to be confident.

RocketLawyer

www.rocketlawyer.com

If you aren't sure where to start with the legalities of running your own business, RocketLawyer provides free forms as well as help with legal documents.

SCORE

www.score.org

If you find yourself in need of mentoring from an entrepreneur who's already been through it all, SCORE can help you find a mentor.

Startup Nation

www.startupnation.com

Startup Nation offers entrepreneurial advice from a whole mix of people who have been there and done that.

SUCCESS Foundation

www.successfoundation.org

This site provides the fundamental principles of personal development and the resources to help you achieve your full potential.

Teenage Love Affair

www.teenageloveaffair.com

Highlights inspirational teens and provides career advice.

TeenLifeBlog

www.teenlife.com

Learn various tips on how to start a business and find template documents to help you.

Udemy

www.udemy.com

Take online public speaking classes in a variety of different professional subjects.

Zoho

www.zoho.com

For a full suite of business tools, including CRM, invoicing, project management, and databases, check out Zoho.

Books

The Self-Esteem Workbook for Teens: Activities to help you build confidence and achieve your goals, by Lisa M. Schab (2013)

Feel the Fear . . . and Do It Anyway: Dynamic techniques for turning fear, indecision, and anger into power, action, and love, by Susan Jeffers (2006)

The Confidence to Be Yourself: How to boost your self-esteem, by Brian Roet (2013)

Index

About the Authors

Please visit *http://fairytalesuccess.tumblr.com* to connect with us and other entrepreneurs following the same path as you!

Adrienne Arieff is the author of *The Sacred Thread* (Crown, 2012) and coauthored *SPA* (Taschen, 2010) and is the principal of Arieff Communications, an integrative marketing and public relations company.

Adrienne has been featured on *CNN*, the *New York Times*, *USA Today*, and the *Today Show*. Adrienne periodically guest lectures on public relations at various conferences and universities.

She managed teen brands for adidas, including the Selena Gomez and Justin Bieber campaign for adidas NEO Label, and works with inner city teens in the Bay Area as a tutor and mentor. Her dream job as a child was to work at UNICEF. She collected coins every Halloween as a child and manifested her first job out of college at UNICEF. She then planned and organized study abroad programs for high school students for several years after being inspired by her travels in her teens.

Adrienne decided to write this book because she has been inspired by the teens she works with and mentors. She wanted to create a guidebook of sorts for them to soar and succeed in their lives.

Beverly West is a freelance author and a developmental editor specializing in popular nonfiction, pop culture, self-help, and memoir. As an author, Bev's bestselling series *Cinematherapy* (400,000 copies in print) has inspired eight sequels, been translated into nine languages, and is a TV show in primetime on WE, Women's Entertainment, now in its eleventh season. Bev's cookbook, *Culinarytherapy, the Girl's Guide to Food for Every Mood*, inspired a weekly syndicated column with *Knight Ridder* and was optioned by Touchstone for development as a show on ABC. Bev's book *What Pets Do While You're at Work*, cowritten with her husband Jason, was a Booksense bestseller.

Bev's most recent title *The Sacred Thread*, cowritten with Adrienne, published by Crown in March 2012, was featured in the *New York Times*, and the *Sunday London Times*. Her next two books, *The Secret Lives of Teen Girls*, written with Evelyn Resh, Director of Sexual Health Services for the Canyon Ranch, published last fall from Hay House, and is now a regular feature on Oprah.com, and *Pure Cute*, from Andrews McMeel, is in its fifth printing.

Bev is an avid home chef, a Fairway Market fanatic, and the hostess of frequent and sometimes notorious dinner parties. Bev lives with her husband Jason and their four dogs, one cat, and two turtles in a third floor walk-up farm on the Upper West Side of Manhattan.